J. Lewis Farley

Egypt, Cyprus and Asiatic Turkey

J. Lewis Farley

Egypt, Cyprus and Asiatic Turkey

ISBN/EAN: 9783743322288

Manufactured in Europe, USA, Canada, Australia, Japa

Cover: Foto ©Andreas Hilbeck / pixelio.de

Manufactured and distributed by brebook publishing software (www.brebook.com)

J. Lewis Farley

Egypt, Cyprus and Asiatic Turkey

EGYPT,

CYPRUS AND ASIATIC TURKEY.

BY

J. LEWIS FARLEY,

KNIGHT GOLD CROSS OF THE SERVIAN ORDER OF THE TAKOVO;
CORRESPONDING MEMBER OF THE INSTITUT EGYPTIEN OF ALEXANDRIA;
AUTHOR OF "THE RESOURCES OF TURKEY,"
"TURKS AND CHRISTIANS,"
ETC., ETC.

LONDON:
TRÜBNER & CO., LUDGATE HILL.
1878.

[The Right of Translation is reserved.]

LONDON:
CLAYTON AND CO., TEMPLE PRINTING WORKS,
BOUVERIE STREET, WHITEFRIARS.

TO THE MANY FRIENDS,

BOTH MUSSULMAN AND CHRISTIAN,

WHOSE KINDNESS AND HOSPITALITY

RENDERED HIS SOJOURN IN SYRIA

SO AGREEABLE,

This Book

IS DEDICATED BY

THE AUTHOR.

PREFACE.

Some explanation is due to the readers of this volume for what may be justly considered the want of continuity in its pages. The fact is that when I commenced the first chapter, my only purpose was to direct attention to the attractions of a winter residence in Egypt, of spring in Syria, and summer on the Bosphorus. As I proceeded, however, I could not fail to remember, what many persons now appear to forget, that Palestine and Syria form part of Asiatic Turkey, and are justly entitled to whatever privileges the convention between Great Britain and the Porte may in the future bring to Asia Minor. Having resided many years in Asiatic Turkey, and given special attention to its resources, and to the deplorable condition of its populations, I felt that the British Protectorate was a subject which I could not well pass by in silence. My views thereon consequently fill a considerable portion of this volume.

Our recent acquisition of Cyprus has also given occasion for a few passing observations. I have visited the island, and resided during two years on the neighbouring coast of Syria; and was, at the time, led to believe that Cyprus was one of the healthiest islands in the Mediterranean. If it has not proved to be so for our troops, the imprudence of the authorities in charge is to be largely blamed.

The future of the Ottoman Empire, and the effect which the British Protectorate may have upon that future, are questions upon which I do not presume to be dogmatic. I trust, however, that my long experience of the country will impart some practical value to my views.

14, *Cockspur Street, Pall Mall, S.W.*,
Nov. 7, 1878.

CONTENTS.

CHAPTER I.

                                                              PAGES.

Winter in Egypt—The land of the Khédive—Alexandria, Cairo, and Suez Canal—Progress of Egypt—Products—Cairo as a winter residence—Climate—Travelling on the Nile—The Dahabeah—The Nile steamer—Ruins of Luxor and Karnak—Dancing girls of Esneh—Cost of journey to Philæ and back ... ... 1—8

CHAPTER II.

Travelling in Palestine and Syria—Mistakes made by travellers—Climate—Most economical way of seeing the country—Tent Life—Beyrout—Remarkable places to visit—Best months in which to visit Palestine and Syria—Beyrout as a *pied-à-terre*—Routes from London ... ... 9—13

CHAPTER III.

Beyrout—Climate—Comparison of the climate of Beyrout with that of Hyères, Nice, Naples and Madeira—Beyrout under the Romans—Its former greatness—Approach to Beyrout by sea—Scenery of Beyrout and Mount Lebanon—Historical

reminiscences—Celebrated places in vicinity—
Society—Cost of living—Advantages of Beyrout
as a health resort—Râs-el-Beyrout—Hôtel de
Belle Vue—Improvements in Beyrout ... ... 14—27

CHAPTER IV.

Beit-Miry on Mount Lebanon—Druses and Maronites
—Scenery—The Plain of Beyrout—The Nahr-el-
Beyrout—Luxuriant vegetation—Brûmanah ... 28—34

CHAPTER V.

Mount Lebanon—Climate—Effect of the climate in
restoring health—Journey to Ghazir, Harîsa,
and Antoura—Cave of St. George—Dog River—
Village of Junêh—Scenery of Mount Lebanon—
Maronite hospitality—Maronite princess—The
tantoor—Arab horses, their training and sagacity—Monastery of Harîsa—Lebanon wine—
Monastery of Beit-Cash-Bow—College of Antoura—Education on Mount Lebanon—Syrian
courtesy—Salutations in various countries—Convent of Deir-Beshâra—The nuns—Village of
Zook—The Nahr-el-Kelb—Dinner at the Hôtel
Pittoresque—The Dog River by moonlight—Return to Beyrout by water ... ... 35—53

CHAPTER VI.

Beyrout to Jerusalem—Jaffa—Plains of Sharon—
Ramleh—Esdouad—Azotus—Gath—Lydda—Ajalon—Kirjath-Jearim—Elah—Emmaus—Bethany—Jericho—The Jordan—Solomon's Pools—
Hebron—Jerusalem—Beyrout to Damascus—

The Damascus Road—Its success—The Beyrout
Water-Works Company—Its failure—Damascus   54—57

CHAPTER VII.

Beyrout to Nazareth—Kaiffa—Mount Carmel—Route from Kaiffa—Plains of Esdraelon—The Bedawîns—Costumes of the people—Convent of Terra Santa—Hospitality of the monks—Church of the Annunciation—The Virgin's well—St. Joseph's workshop—Scenery round Nazareth—Associations—Cana of Galilee—Mount of Beatitudes—Tiberias—Mount Tabor—The monk's dream—Church of the Transfiguration—Plains of Zabulon   ...   .   58—67

CHAPTER VIII.

A day with the Bedawîns—The tribe of the Hawâras—Salihl-Aga—The village of Abilîn—Marriage festivities—Breakfast with a Bedawîn Chief—Arab hospitality—Sham-fight—Casting the djerreed—The Bridegroom—Fight for the love-token—Arab customs—Dancers—Ride to St. Jean d'Acre—Fortifications—Mount Carmel—Convent of St. Elias   68—75

CHAPTER IX.

Syria—Ancient Syria—The Phœnicians—Tyre—Syria under the Romans—Under the Khalifs—Wealth and splendour of its cities—Occupation by the Turks—Mussulman and Turk not synonymous terms—The Arabs—Civilization of the Mussulman East—The Moors in Spain—Superiority of the Arab race—The Arab and his Turkish masters—Desire for independence—The restoration of the Holy Land—Syria and Palestine as a field for immigration—Commercial improvement —Future importance of Beyrout ... ... 76—85

CHAPTER X.

The British Protectorate of Asiatic Turkey—Lord Beaconsfield and the Empire of the East—What is the British Protectorate?—Reforms—The Turkish Pashas—Fuad and Midhat—Regeneration of Asiatic Turkey—Internal administration— Turkish justice—The judges and the local councils—The elective principle—Collection of taxes —The usurer, tax-farmer, and Turkish officials —Condition of the agricultural population—Difficulties of the task undertaken by the British Government... ... ... 86—106

CHAPTER XI.

The resources of Asiatic Turkey—Mineral wealth— Coal mines of Heraclia—The valleys of Kosloo and Soungoul—Metalliferous minerals—Copper mines of Eléon, Bakyrkurchai, Tireboli, Argana-Madén, and Tokat—Silver mines of Gumush-Khaneh—Lead and silver mines of Balgar-Dagh, Akdagh-Madén, Esseli, Kuré-Madén, and Helveli—Agricultural resources—Area of Turkey in Asia—Syria, Palestine, and Asia Minor as a field for immigration—Hints to immigrants— Visit to a model farm—Profits on grain-farming

CONTENTS.   xiii

                                                   PAGES.

—Sheep—Vine culture and wine-making—The
mulberry and rearing of silkworms—Asiatic
Turkey as a field for British capital and enterprise—Public works—The future of Syria, Palestine and Asia Minor   ...   . 107—120

CHAPTER XII.

Railways in Asiatic Turkey—Defective appliances for
the transport of merchandize—Narrow-gauge
railways—The Smyrna and Aidin Railway—The
Smyrna and Cassaba—The Varna and Rustchuk
—Roads—Samsoun, Sivas, Angora, and Sinope
—Anatolia—The Trebizond road—The Persian
transit trade—Railway from Batoum *vid* Kars
to Tabreez—Harbours—Canalization of rivers
—Smyrna—Beyrout—Jaffa—The desideratum
for Asiatic Turkey ...   . 121—132

CHAPTER XIII.

The Euphrates Valley Railway—Mr. W. P. Andrew's
project—Mr. Latham's project—The great scheme
of Sir Macdonald Stephenson—Cost of Mr. Andrew's projected railway—Practicability of the
Euphrates Valley route—Superiority of the Tigris route over that of the Euphrates Valley—
Alexandretta—Aleppo—The grand idea of Sir
Macdonald Stephenson—Railway from the Bosphorus to the Persian Gulf—Cost of the railway—
Distance from the Straits of Dover to Bussorah
—Relative merits of the different schemes—Proposed routes—Dividend-paying value of the
traffic   ...   . 133—148

CHAPTER XIV.

Beyrout to Cyprus—Larnaca—Famagûsta—Siege by the Turks—Fate of Marcantonio Bragadino—Population of Cyprus—Uncultivated land in Cyprus—Products—Mineral and agricultural resources—Archæology—Health of the Island—Sickness of British troops caused by imprudence and want of ordinary precautions—Best preventatives against intermittent fever—Suggestions to our Government—Public works ... ... 149—154

CHAPTER XV.

The island of Cyprus—Its area—Soil—Agriculture—Products—Mineral products—Salt-pits—Manufactures—Ports—Roads—Commerce—Population—Condition of the inhabitants ... ... 155—164

CHAPTER XVI.

Cyprus to Constantinople—Rhodes—The Knights of St. John—Patmos—Cos—Samos—Scio—Smyrna—Ruins of Ephesus—Climate and society of Smyrna—Mitylene—Lesbos—Tenedos—Dardanelles—The site of Homeric Troy ... ... 165—171

CHAPTER XVII.

Summer on the Bosphorus—First view of Constantinople—Improvements in Stamboul—Galata and Pera—Hotels—Salubrity of Constantinople—The ancient Byzantium—Oracle of Apollo—Chalcedon—The Emperor Constantine—The Eastern Empire—Last of the Palæologi—The fall of Con-

stantinople—Mohammed II.—The Crescent and the
Star—Constantine the Great—Extent of the
Eastern Empire—Winter and summer in Con-
stantinople—The Bosphorus—Climate and scenery
—Palaces of the Sultan—The palace of Beylerbey
—Prinkipo and Buyukderé—Sweet Waters of
Europe and Asia—Scutari—The Giant's Mountain
—Turkish women, their status and treatment—
The laws of the Koran in reference to women—
Objects of interest to be seen in Constantinople
—Mosque of Saint Sophia—The Hasné, or
Imperial treasury—The bazaars—Howling and
Dancing Dervishes—The Sultan going to Mosque
—Routes from Constantinople to London ... 172—192

CHAPTER XVIII.

The future of the Ottoman Empire—Tradition of the
Turks—Retirement of the Turks to Asia—Deci-
sions of the Berlin Congress—Dismemberment
of Turkey—The Osmanlis as conquerors—Their
decline—Support of the Turks by successive
British Governments—The integrity of Turkey
—The Grand Hellenic Idea—Disappointment of
Greece—Independence of Servia, Montenegro,
and Roumania—Detachment of Bulgaria, Bosnia,
Herzegovina, and the Dobrudsha—Austria and
the Slaves—Struggle between the Slaves and the
Greeks—Constantinople, the future capital of a
Greek or Slavonic Empire—The British Protec-
torate of Asiatic Turkey—Probable complications
—Promises of reform by the Sultan—The Turkish
Pashas—Reformation of Asiatic Turkey by the

British Government—Asia Minor—Aspirations of the people of Palestine and Syria—The acquisition of Cyprus—Its future—Annexation of Palestine, Syria and Asia Minor to Great Britain—Our Indian Empire—Afghanistan—Persia—Future of Asiatic Turkey ... ... 193—217

APPENDICES.

I. The Suez Canal ... ... 219—227
II. Fuad Pasha's Political Testament ... ... 228—245
III. Law Granting to Foreigners the Right of Holding Real Property in the Ottoman Empire ... 246—254
IV. The Trade of Cyprus ... ... 255—263

EGYPT, CYPRUS, AND ASIATIC TURKEY.

CHAPTER I.

WINTERING IN EGYPT.

The land of the Khédive is likely soon to rival in greatness the ancient Kingdom of the Pharaohs and the Ptolemies. Modern Egypt cannot, it is true, compare with ancient Egypt in the number of its inhabitants or the splendour of its cities;* but what successive sovereigns, from Sesostris to the Khalifs, failed to effect, or accomplished only in part, has been completely achieved, under the rule of the Khédive, by the opening of the Suez Canal,† while Alexandria and Cairo are fast becoming cities of palaces, and the wealth of the country itself is every day increasing.

* Herodotus tells us that in the reign of Amasis there were 20,000 cities in Egypt, while Diodorus says that in his time there were 30,000 towns and villages.
† See "Suez Canal," Appendix I.

Western prejudice attributes the present ignorance of the Mussulman population of Turkey to Islamism, and concludes that the religion of Mahommed is a bar to all human progress. Any one, however, who visited Egypt fifteen years ago, and could now see the vast improvements that have been, and are still being made by the Khédive, would at once have his prejudices very much modified, if not altogether removed. He would see the harbour of Alexandria, the finest, probably, in the world, crowded with the shipping of all nations; with a new breakwater and new docks in course .of completion; warehouses filled with cotton, grain, and other agricultural produce, ready for export; railways in operation or in course of construction; everywhere, in fact, the signs of increasing civilization and prosperity. He would see Alexandria itself more like an European than an Eastern city, with its magnificent buildings and its "Place des Consuls," that exceeds in size and beauty any square to be found in Europe. He would see the land irrigated by the Nile's overflow, or by means of machinery, everywhere teeming with rich crops of wheat, maize, barley, beans, and peas; clover and flax; rice, sugarcane, tobacco, and cotton; coffee, indigo, and madder; the gardens producing apricots in May; peaches, plums, apples, pears, and caroubs in June; grapes, figs, and prickly pears in July; pomegranates, lemons, and dates in August; oranges in October; sweet lemons and bananas in November; and the mulberry and Seville orange in January. In old times, we know, there was "corn in Egypt;" now there is also "cotton in Egypt," and cotton, too, of the best description. Even ten years ago, there were not less than two hundred steam ploughs at work in cotton cultivation. Every mechanical aid to production has, in fact, been made use of, and the result is an enormous increase of wealth both to the people and their ruler.

The long sea passage deterred many persons from visiting Egypt; but now that the journey from Brindisi to Alexandria can be made in three days and a half, the superiority of Lower Egypt over the South of France or Italy as a winter residence will become better known and appreciated. Cairo is, *par excellence*, the most perfect Arab city of the present day, and one in which its inhabitants have, perhaps, attained to a higher degree of civilization than in any other city in the East. The climate of Egypt is salubrious during the greater part of the year, and in Alexandria, even the heat of summer is seldom oppressive, being tempered by a fresh northerly breeze. The Khamseen, or hot south wind, however, which prevails in April and May, is at times unpleasant; and the inundations from the Nile render the latter part of the autumn less healthy than the summer and winter. In summer, the village of Ramléh, four miles from Alexandria, is a charming residence; while Cairo, from its clear, dry atmosphere and equable temperature, is now admitted to be one of the most desirable winter resorts for invalids. The Khédive, too, who, from his immense wealth, his splendid hospitality, and liberal patronage of art, is justly entitled to be called the Haroun-al-Raschid of modern times, is fast rendering his capital as luxurious as it is interesting.

One of the principal advantages which invalids derive from a winter's residence in a favourable climate, is that they are enabled to take daily and efficient exercise in the open air. At Cairo, the invalid or tourist can be constantly in the open air, either on foot, donkey-back, horseback, or in a carriage. The atmosphere is not subject to any sudden change, nor is there danger of vicissitudes of temperature such as are experienced in many places in the South of Europe, nor cold cutting winds such as frequently prevail during winter and spring at Nice and Naples. The complete change, too, from the habits and customs of Western Europe to those of an Eastern city like Cairo, is, I am convinced, of immense importance to valetudinarians, for impressions made upon the mind react upon the body, and the novelty of the new style of life in Egypt gradually weans one from a too-frequent thought of self. Who could think of dyspepsia or hypochondriasis while beholding the lovely sunrises and glorious sunsets, which in our foggy and comparatively dismal climate are never seen, or while contemplating, as at Thebes, the ruins of a civilization that existed long before Athens and Rome were founded, or the history of Greece had even been begun?

The pleasantest months for a residence at Cairo are December, January, and February. The inundations of the Nile, having subsided, leave the fields in November covered with a fresh layer of rich deposit; then the lands are put under cultivation; and during our winter months, which are, in fact, the spring months in Egypt, the Delta, as well as the

Valley of the Nile, looks like a delightful garden, teeming with verdure, and beautiful with the blossoms of trees and plants. It very seldom rains at Cairo, probably not more than three or four times in the year. Dr. Abbot records a few drops of rain on December 26; slight rain, January 25; heavy rain, January 30; a few drops, February 9 and 16; and a few drops, March 6 and 14. The thermometer, on the average, in the month of December, ranges from 56° to 64° at 9 A.M., and from 68° to 77° in the afternoon. In January, 52° to 69°, and 64° to 79°. In February, 56° to 69°, and 65° to 75°. In March, 60° to 76°, and 60° to 78°.

The romance of travel in Egypt is, however, fast disappearing. A new bridge has been recently built over the Nile, by the Khédive, so that travellers can now go direct in carriages from their hotel to the Pyramids without being obliged, as formerly, to cross the river in boats, and finish the excursion on camels or donkeys. The old 'Dahabeah,' or Nile boat, is giving way to the comparatively luxurious Nile steamer; and the charms of that dreamy Epicurean life, floating up and down the great river, will soon become a memory of the past. No more encampments beneath the myriad stars and the wondrous sky of an Egyptian night, amidst the labyrinth of pillars, obelisks, and fallen temples of Luxor or Karnak. Instead of, as heretofore, passing the night on land under a tent, the traveller now sleeps in his comfortable berth on board the Khédive's steamer, and "does" the Nile in three weeks instead of three months, as in the palmy days of the Dahabeahs. Before the steamers began to ply, the price for a first-class boat was from £90 to £120 a month, for three months; while now the voyage —585 miles, from Cairo to Philæ, a few miles above the First Cataract—and back again, can be made at a cost of £44, including steamer, living, guides, and all other necessary expenses. Of course, those who have plenty of time and money at their disposal can have no difficulty in obtaining Dahabeahs, if they prefer that mode of locomotion; but to such as are limited in these respects, the steamers will be found more convenient. The latter are small, carrying from fourteen to seventeen passengers, and stop at all the places worth seeing between Cairo and the First Cataract—viz., Beni-Swaif, Minyéh, Beni-Hassan, Syout, Girgeh, Keneh, Luxor, Karnak, Esneh, Edfou, Koam-Embou, and Assouan. A day and a half is spent at Assouan and Philæ, and three days at Luxor and Karnak.

My readers would not, I am certain, thank me for a description of Cairo, its squares, streets, mosques, and bazaars; for has not each remarkable spot in that famed Arab city been "done" over and over again by book-making travellers of every stamp? Has not every one, too, gazed in imagination on the Sphinx, and ascended the Great Pyramid, that covers an area equal to the entire of Lincoln's Inn Fields, and is one-third higher than the ball of St. Paul's? Have not the Ghawazes, or dancing-girls, of Esneh been pictured in glowing words, and painted on undying canvas? And have not the wonders of Thebes, "the city with a hundred gates," and all the temples, colossi, sphinxes, obelisks, and tombs of Luxor, Karnak, Philæ, Syout, Abydos, and Dendera been made familiar by Heeren, Lepsius, Kenrick, Wilkinson, and Gliddon? My object is not to describe the scenery of the Nile, but simply to direct attention to the climatic advantages of Egypt, and to Cairo, the city of the Khédive, as a suitable winter residence.

CHAPTER II.

TRAVELLING IN SYRIA.

No one who has passed the winter in Egypt should return to Europe without, if possible, visiting Syria and Palestine; and, in my opinion, the pleasantest months for doing so are March, April, and May.* In autumn, the country is parched by the scorching sun of July, August, and September; but in spring, everything, refreshed by the rains of January and February, looks green and pleasant. Nature is then seen in her most brilliant aspect, while the temperature corresponds to that of a fine English summer.

A great mistake, however, which most travellers have hitherto made when visiting the Holy Land is in following the old beaten track

---

* The French steamers leave Alexandria in the evening, and arrive at Jaffa on the following morning. Starting again about 4 P.M. they reach Beyrout at daybreak.

by first landing at Jaffa; thence, *viâ* Ramleh, to Jerusalem; from Jerusalem, by Nablous and Samaria, to Nazareth; from Nazareth to Tiberias and Damascus; from Damascus to Baalbek; and from Baalbek to Beyrout. This journey occupies about five weeks; but although it has many attractions, and possesses, for the romantically inclined, an indescribable charm, it has, on the other hand, many disadvantages. The wandering life, from day to day, under a pure and cloudless sky, and the encampment at night, on the brow of a hill, or in some sheltered valley, beneath the dome-like vault of heaven, are replete with pleasurable sensations unknown to the tourist in Europe; but there are many incidental drawbacks, not the least being the fatigue which every one has not the strength to bear. Tent-life, for those who enjoy physical strength and mental energy, accompanied by a spirit of adventure and enterprise, is certainly very delightful; but not at all suited to ladies or invalids. Another disadvantage is the difficulty of thoroughly examining the country, and becoming perfectly acquainted with the manners, habits, and customs of the people. The dragoman generally agrees that the journey shall be completed within a specified number of days. He is bound to supply tents, food, servants, horses, and everything actually necessary; for this he receives a certain sum per head, as mentioned in the contract which is signed and sealed at the British Consulate. It is, therefore, his interest to finish the journey within a stipulated time; and thus many lovely spots out of the beaten track are unobserved, and many opportunities for enjoying the beauties of nature are lost. Moreover, the inconvenience and anxiety, particularly with ladies, attached to carrying a quantity of luggage from place to place, are very great; and the expense, unless where the party is numerous, becomes considerable.

The most economical, and, from my own experience, the pleasantest way of seeing the country, is for the tourist to establish his head-quarters at Beyrout, as excursions can thence be made to the most interesting places in Syria and Palestine at a comparatively trifling cost, and with little or no fatigue. The Hôtel de Belle Vue, on the sea-shore, a short distance from the town, is, in every respect, excellent; the apartments are clean, the food unexceptionable, and the attendance all that could be desired. The air is pure and refreshing; the house commands an uninterrupted view of the Mediterranean; while, on the right, looking from the balcony, over Beyrout and Saint George's Bay, there is a picture of surpassing loveliness which I have never seen exceeded. Frequent excursions can be made to Mount Lebanon. The celebrated palace of Bteddîn, built by the Emir Beeher, is only six hours', and the villages of Beit-Miry and Brûmanah, two hours' distance from Beyrout. The Nahr-el-Kelb—Dog River—is two hours by land, or an hour and a half by water. The route to Baalbek lies, for some way, along the new Damascus road, and the famed "City of the Sun" can now be reached with little difficulty. Zahleh, Zibdany, Djezzin, and Deir-el-Kamr, in the southern, or "mixed districts" inhabited by Druses and Maronites, are also well worth a visit. The scenery of the Kesrawân, or northern portion of the Lebanon, inhabited exclusively by Maronites, is, however, not at all inferior to that of the Druse districts, and the hospitality offered in the numerous monasteries to be met with in this part of the mountain renders travelling there more easy and agreeable.

The months of March, April, and May can

be very agreeably spent by making the Hôtel de Belle Vue one's *pied-à-terre*, and visiting, from time to time, the various places of interest in the neighbourhood.

CHAPTER III.

BEYROUT.

It has often been to me a matter for surprise that, considering the number of persons who yearly seek the South of France or Italy for the benefit of their health, so few choose Syria as a residence. The climate, particularly of Beyrout, is superior to many places in Europe frequented by invalids; while, for those predisposed to pulmonary complaints, it affords advantages that can hardly be found elsewhere. Hyères has long enjoyed the reputation of being an excellent locality for persons suffering from bronchial affections; yet it is much exposed to the *mistral*, in consequence of the absence of protecting hills on the north-west, and in winter, spring, and autumn, cold north-easterly winds prevail to a considerable extent. Nice has enjoyed a still higher celebrity, although the inconstancy of the winds is very great—the temperature being subject to violent changes which are extremely trying to delicate or nervous organizations. The invalid is tempted out of doors by a brilliant sun, and then attacked by a cold piercing wind that neither clothes nor flannel can keep out. Dr. Meryon, who passed a season at Nice, declares that "there are more natives who die of consumption at Nice than in any town in England of the same amount of population." Naples, although possessing many advantages, cannot boast much of its climate, which is exceedingly changeable during winter. Cold cutting winds prevail in the spring, while the sirocco, by its relapsing and paralyzing influence, renders persons incapable, during its continuance, of either mental or bodily exertion. Even Madeira, which has long been considered the paradise of invalids, is not so favourably situated as is popularly supposed. Drs. Heineken and Gourlay, who practised in the island, state that no disease was more common among the native population than consumption; and Dr. Mason says that "affections of the digestive organs are a frequent cause of death with the majority of the inhabitants, and there are few places where the system is more liable to general disorder."

The climate of Beyrout, on the contrary, is always moderate, and subject to less change than any of those places I have named. Asthma, bronchitis, and pulmonary disorders are unknown; the temperature is not subject to sudden vicissitudes of cold and heat; and the wind, from whatever quarter it may blow, never possesses any bleakness or ungenial chill. January and February are the only unpleasant months in the year, as then the heavy rains come on; but the air is always balmy, and the blue sky is seldom obscured for any considerable length of time. March, April, and May are delightful months, as all nature, refreshed by the showers, looks bright and cheerful; the "green herb and the emerald grass" are once more renewed, the cactus overhangs the roads with its clustering blossoms, and the orange-tree puts forth its chaste and simple flower, loading the air with perfume. The months of July, August, and September are very hot in Beyrout; but the vicinity of Mount Lebanon affords means of varying the temperature to any extent that may be desired. Some of the foreign residents remain in Beyrout during the entire summer, but the greater number send their families to the villages of Beit-Miry, Brûmanah, or Shemlîn. Beit-

Miry is distant about one hour and a half, Brûmanah two, and Shemlîn five hours. October, November, and December are like May in England.

Beyrout is a place of great antiquity, and became of considerable importance under the Roman emperors. Justinian called it the Nurse of the Law, and conferred on it the privilege of teaching Roman jurisprudence in its schools. Traces of the magnificent baths and theatre, erected by Agrippa, were to be seen, some few years ago, on the north of the town; and even now, portions of tesselated pavement and columns of perfect finish are found in the gardens and on the sea-shore. The Romans gave the name of Felix to the city, and, after its destruction by Tryphon, it was rebuilt by Augustus, who thought it worthy to bear the name of his favourite daughter Julia.

The view of Beyrout, as the traveller approaches from the sea, is very fine.* While

---

* There are three routes by which travellers can reach Beyrout from London:—First, *viâ* Brindisi to Alexandria, and thence by steamer. Second, *viâ* Vienna to Trieste, and then by the Austrian Lloyd's line of packets. Third, *viâ* Paris to Marseilles, and thence by French steamer.

c

still at a distance, the peaks of Mount Lebanon are seen in mid-air, surrounded by the bold outline of its undulating ridges. Gradually the outline becomes more and more distinct. Vast ravines are seen between the chasms that divide rock from rock, and huge masses loom forth like sudden creations out of chaos. Specks appear on the mountain side that presently expand into hamlets and villages; while, on higher points, the towers of numerous monasteries stand aloft in bold relief against the sky. The mountainous surface of the interior slowly spreads out like a diorama, and, as the steamer holds her way, the scene seems to unfold itself as if by enchantment. The houses scattered over the plain gleam in the morning sun from amidst their surrounding foliage, and the breeze from the shore comes laden with sweets from groves of citron and orange. To the left, in the distance, is the snow-capped summit of Jebel-Sunnin;* and, in front, Beyrout herself, charmingly situated on the slope of a hill, her head, as it were, in the clouds, her feet bathed by the sea. The

---

* *Jebel* . . Mountain.   *Deir* . . Monastery.
  Nahr . . River.   *Ras*. . . Cape.

houses, with their slender arches and flat roofs, surmounted with embrasures of stone or balustrades of wood; the picturesque rocks along the shore; the white-mulberry gardens and orange and citron groves; the terraces filled with flowers; the palms towering towards the sky; the various and lively colours of the walls; the minarets of the mosques; the grand and noble mountain; the atmosphere serene and bright;—all blend into a picture the most beautiful I ever beheld.

There are few places that can compete with Beyrout in the various inducements which it offers both to the traveller and the invalid. The country all round is historical. There is scarcely a spot on which the foot treads, or over which the eye wanders, that is not rich in the brilliant memories of the past. Cyprus, on the one side, recalls the classic days of old, when the lovely goddess arose out of the sea at Paphos; Tyre, on the other, awakens visions of princely argosies at anchor beneath marble palaces stretching to the water's edge. Farther on is Acre,—before the mind's eye the Red Cross of the Crusader sinks beneath the Crescent of Salah-ed-dîn. Opposite is Carmel, whose "flowery top perfumes the skies;" and six hours thence is Nazareth, Mount Tabor, and Genesareth. Twelve hours from Beyrout is Damascus the beautiful; Baalbek is but forty miles distant; the Druse and Maronite villages of Mount Lebanon are in the vicinity; a visit to the Cedars forms a pleasant excursion; while the Nahr-el-Kelb and cave of St. George are only an afternoon's ride.

Life and property are perfectly secure in Beyrout. Murder, robbery, and other crimes so frequent in European cities, are nearly unknown, and a visitor might travel over all the surrounding country without the least danger of molestation. During my residence in Beyrout, I rented a small house for the months of May and June, completely isolated on the borders of the Little Desert, and a considerable distance from any European habitation. My horse was picketed at night in the open air; my servant went home in the evening to his family, and I slept with much more security, than I should, probably, have done under similar circumstances in the suburbs of London. I have often, too, ridden by moonlight, attended only by an Arab groom, from the Nahr-el-Kelb to Beyrout; and, at other times, from Beyrout to Beit-Miry with, certainly, no fear, and, decidedly, more safety than in many rural districts in England.

The society of Beyrout, although limited, is agreeable. The foreign residents are very hospitable; many of the married ladies having a special evening in each week for receptions. There are two principal hotels; one in the town, the other, some little distance on the shore, at Râs-el-Beyrout. The latter, although not comparable with English hotels, is exceedingly clean and comfortable. The terms are ten shillings per day, wine of Lebanon included. Rents vary from twenty-five to sixty pounds a year, and furniture of a plain description is easily procured. Servants' wages are—for a good cook about two pounds, and a groom (Egyptians are the best) twenty-five shillings a month. A serviceable horse may be purchased for eight to twelve pounds, and, as barley is cheap, it can be kept for about two pounds per month. The necessaries of life are all very moderate.*

Those animals that minister to the wants of man are abundant. The goats are large, and yield milk of superior quality. The sheep attain

---

* Now that Beyrout is becoming a sanitarium for our troops at Cyprus, the cost of living will no doubt increase.

an unusual size, and their tails, terminating in a ball of fat, become so heavy that they can hardly drag them along; their flesh is excellent. Fish and game are plentiful. Grouse, partridge, snipe, quail, and wild duck are abundant in the season. Vegetables of every description,—beans, peas, lettuces, onions, melons, cucumbers, &c. The gardens are filled with the citron and orange. Aleppo sends the far-famed pistachio to market. Jaffa produces the delicious watermelon; Damascus,—plums, cherries, peaches, and, above all, the apricot, called, by the Persians, the Seed of the Sun. In short, everything is there in profusion to satisfy material wants, to soothe the senses, and charm the imagination. In its ethereal atmosphere, mere existence becomes enjoyment, for you have only to live to be happy; only to open your eyes to behold the brightest sky and loveliest landscapes; only to stretch out your hand to pluck the sweetest and fairest flowers, and gather the most delicate and luscious fruits.

To the stranger, everything in Beyrout contrasts remarkably with what he has been accustomed to in Europe. The Maronite, Armenian, and Druse; the Turk, Greek, and

Arab; the Bedawîns, with their picturesque costume and wild restless eye; the novel phases of Eastern life daily seen in the bazaars;—all afford an ever-changing scene of amusement. In nothing, however, is the contrast greater than in the climate. November in London and November in Beyrout; from damp and fog, and copper-coloured stifling vapour, to blue sky, clear atmosphere, and bright sunshine.

> "If all were free,
> Who would not, like the swallow, flit, and find
> What season suited him? In summer heats
> Wing northward; and in winter build his home
> In sheltered valleys nearer to the sun."

Syria has manifold attractions; but, after all, her great charm is the sun. Until you visit the East, you can hardly say you have ever seen the sun; comparatively, there is but twilight elsewhere. In Syria, you see and feel it; your heart is, as it were, filled with it—it is reflected everywhere. All your sensations give token of the change; and every feeling, every thought becomes brighter and gayer. The cares which may have hitherto beset you appear to be lifted from off your heart; you feel raised above the earth, and breathe, in reality, the air of heaven. There is no glare, for the sun shines with a soft and mellow light that makes the landscape look as if it calmly slept. No wonder the Parsees worshipped him.

The favourite walk is to the west of the town, along the sea-shore at Râs-el-Beyrout. There, at the various *cafés*, the pedestrian can observe the picturesque costumes of the people, as they sip their coffee or inhale the fragrant tobacco of Djebail; some seated at the doors, others reclining on the grass, or on the rocks overhanging the sea,—everywhere forming groups the most various and picturesque. The hotel, I have already mentioned, is situated on the Râs-el-Beyrout, and thence, towards evening, one of the finest views of the town and mountains may be obtained.

> "Now upon Syria's land of roses
> Softly the light of eve reposes,
> And, like a glory, the broad sun
> Hangs over sainted Lebanon;
> Whose head in wintry grandeur towers,
> And whitens with eternal sleet;
> While Summer, in a vale of flowers,
> Is sleeping rosy at his feet."

At this hour, nothing can exceed the beauty of the view. To the west, the sky is one sheet of burnished gold, shedding its brightness for miles over the waters. Here and there, the descending sun throws streaks of light across the many-coloured houses of Beyrout, and beyond, the varied and ever-changing tints of the mountains,—now bright green, now purple; at one moment, the deep gorges revealed to the eye, the next lost in impenetrable shade; here the monasteries standing out in bold relief, there lost to view as if by magic,—all form a picture which even Poussin or Claude Lorraine has never realized. Passing the Hôtel de Belle Vue, a narrow path winds along the rocky shore until, arriving at the potteries, it becomes wider, and then forms a delightful promenade to the extreme point of Râs-el-Beyrout where the cliff rises two hundred feet above the level of the sea. The walk is pleasantly varied by proceeding over the sands and through the winding lanes, bordered by the cactus and numerous flowering shrubs, to the Grande Place and the barracks, whence there is a beautiful view, overlooking the town, St. George's Bay, the Nahr-Beyrout, and Lebanon. Often, from this barrack hill, have I admired the wonderful light and shade on the mountains, and the various changes in the colour of the sea. In the morning, the mountain casts its immense shadow over the waves, which then appear of a deep blue, lightly tipped with foam; at mid-day, they are like billows of gold in the distance, and silver in the foreground; in the evening, when the breeze lulls and the sun declines, the sea is one vast mirror, where the gigantic forms of the mountains are drawn with a softness of shading and distinctness of outline most remarkable and perfect. Then, as the sun sinks more and more, the waves change from blue to violet, from violet to purple, through every gradation of colour, until, at length, darkness comes with tropical suddenness upon the scene, and all is wrapped in gloom.

As I have said of Cairo, so also it can be said of Beyrout, that the great benefit which an invalid may derive from a residence there is the facility of taking constant exercise in the open air. The early morning walk, when the birds begin their song, is healthful and invigorating; the sun is not then too powerful; the air is cool, and the flowers, refreshed by the dew, give forth an exquisite perfume. In the afternoon, again, about two hours before sunset, a breeze from the west springs up, and then every one is on horse-back or donkey-back in the Pine Forest,—the Rotten Row of Beyrout. Dr. Lee, whose works on the climate are well known, says, "A principal advantage which invalids derive from a winter's residence in a favourable climate is that they are enabled to take daily and sufficient exercise in the open air; which, by causing free expansion of the lungs, by improving the functions of digestion, and exciting those of the skin to greater activity than would be the case in persons who remained indoors, as also by inducing a more cheerful tone of mind, tends materially to rectify any abnormal condition of the blood, and by these means, better than any other, to obviate the consequences of such abnormal condition when they have not been allowed to proceed too far." The climate of Beyrout appears to me to fulfil all these requirements for the invalid, as its mildness and beauty attract him constantly into the open air; and, when not walking nor on horseback, he can sit on the terrace of his hotel, or on the rocks overlooking the mountains, lulled into a peaceful and delicious reverie by the low murmur of the tideless sea.

CHAPTER IV.

BEIT-MIRY.

BEIT-MIRY, one of the "mixed villages" of Mount Lebanon—inhabited by Druses and Maronites—is the favourite summer resort of the European residents of Beyrout. During the months of July, August, and September, when the heat in the plains is excessive, a sojourn, even for a few weeks, at Beit-Miry is of great advantage to health. The air, particularly at night, is cool and invigorating, and the change of temperature bracing and agreeable. The scenery, too, all round this part of the mountain is grand and impressive. Deep ravines and rising eminences on all sides, the latter clothed with the richest vegetation;—the fig and the olive; the oak and the cedar; the fir-tree and the aloe; the citron and orange; the mulberry and the vine. The paths over the hills are flanked with the vine and fig-tree, which flourish in wild luxuriance, without any assistance from man. Often, when riding from Beit-Miry to Brûmanah, I have plucked the clustering grapes from branches so closely festooned overhead as to almost shut out the sun at mid-day. Even in more elevated parts of Mount Lebanon, where nature seems to afford nothing for the sustenance of the people, numerous Christian villages flourish, and every inch of ground is utilized. Fruit-trees, mulberry plantations, vineyards, and fields of grain abound, though there is scarcely a natural plain of twenty feet square to be seen. The inhabitants, however, meet this difficulty by building terraces, and thus, while retaining the water requisite to irrigate their crops, secure a portion of level ground sufficient to prevent the earth being swept down by the winter rains. By dint of skill and labour, the Maronites have compelled a rocky soil to become fertile. To avail themselves of the waters, they have made channels by means of a thousand windings on the declivities, or arrested the streams by embankments and reservoirs in the valleys. At other places, they have propped up the earth by terraces and walls, so that the mountain presents the appearance of a staircase or amphitheatre, each tier of which is a row of vines or mulberry trees, and of which one hundred to one hundred and twenty tiers may be counted from the bottom to the top of a hill.

It is enchanting to sit upon the brow of a hill at Beit-Miry, sheltered from the sun by a fig-tree or vine, and contemplate the sublimity of nature apparent on every side.

> "For now the noonday quiet holds the hill:
> The grasshopper is silent in the grass:
> The lizard, with his shadow on the stone,
> Rests like a shadow, and the cicala sleeps,
> The purple flowers droop: the golden bee
> Is lily-cradled."

To the west, the plain of Beyrout stretches out before the eye, covered with the orange, the date, the pomegranate, and the banana; the palms, here and there, rearing their tall stems and slender branches in the air; the pines, so dark and solemn, contrasting with the bright colour of the sands; the hills around rising higher and higher, dotted with villages and monasteries; and to the north, the Jebel-Sunnin rearing its snowy crest towards heaven. Few places, indeed, can surpass that glorious plain of Beyrout. There is the orange-tree, whose flowers have been compared to silver, and its fruit to gold; the fig, with its foliage of glossy velvet; the plane, with its rich and brilliant bark; the luxuriant growth of the pine; the graceful flexibility of the palm; the rich verdure of the humbler plants, and prairies bright with the colours, and fragrant with the scent of hyacinths, anemones, and gilly-flowers. Beyond are the hills, with their varying tints, their contrasts of light and shade; afar off is the sea, with its glittering wave-crests and deep azure, reflecting on its surface every hue that fleets over the sky; while, standing out in bold relief against the clear horizon, are the frowning masses of the mountains bounding the prospect in the distance. Towards evening, when the wind sets in from the sea, a curious phenomenon, forming the most exquisite dissolving views, is sometimes observable at Beit-Miry. Vast layers and wreaths of cloudy mist arise from the waters and the plains, and, as they increase, unite, and thicken, they take the appearance of irregular accumulations of foam, or enormous heaps of wool that Titans, or Cyclops, or some fabled giants might be supposed to have shorn from multitudinous flocks, numerous as the sands on the sea-shore. Everything beneath is hidden from sight. After a time, these misty clouds descend gradually as they arose;—the hills and trees, villages and monasteries, appearing to rise up out of a sea of foam, as if in the magical phantasmagoria of a dream.

In some of the valleys near Beit-Miry, the vegetation is so thick, and so completely covers the sloping sides, that it seems as if the very mountains were alive with herbage and verdure. An intermingled mass of fragrant plants, shrubs of delicate foliage, bunches of heather, and tufts of fern, are twined together with innumerable creepers, whose tendrils stretch everywhere and cling where they extend, their festoons hanging from branch to branch or from stone to stone; while, here and there, the ivy mats itself into a thick green coating up the side of the rock. In some places are little spots covered with lichens, growing in one dense mass,—the ground often covered a foot deep with a soft and close vegetable carpet, varied with every shade and hue, and far surpassing, in vividness and beauty, the fantastically-figured fabrics of Turkish looms. All through the valleys, too, spring up, in wild profusion, the most beautiful flowers, whose lively colours and exquisite perfume diversify the landscape and embalm the atmosphere. The myrtle and oleander are there substitutes for our holly and thistles. The hyacinths, jonquils, and tulips fill the parterres; the lilies, so extolled in Scripture for their purity; the anemone, said by the poets to have sprung, near this very spot, from the blood of Adonis; and the narcissi,—

> "The fairest among them all,
> Who gaze on their eyes in the stream's recess
> Till they die of their own dear loveliness."

Each feature of the landscape seen from Beit-Miry is lovely and sublime in itself, and all taken together make up one fascinating and incomparable tableau. The diversified surface of plain, valley, and mountain, with every variety of light and shade, every possible tint and colour of foliage and of rock, every form of tree and herbage; the river of Beyrout wandering like a shiny serpent through the vale; the wide expanse of sea; the eternal and stupendous mass of Lebanon, with its crags and forests; the snowy peaks that shoot up and gleam in the sun like silvery steeples; the joyous though inarticulate voice of birds, and the hum of innumerable insects; the distant lowing of kine, and the strange bleat

D

of the camel; the vast azure canopy of the firmament, against which the crags of the mountain, and the giant trees that seem to emulate the hills, are all mixed and blended into a gorgeous scene that might be taken for fairyland.

CHAPTER V.

MOUNT LEBANON.

The southern portion of Mount Lebanon, called the Choucfat, the Chouf, and the Meten,—"mixed districts," inhabited by Druses and Maronites—is that generally visited by travellers. The Kesrawân, or northern portion, inhabited exclusively by Maronites, is less known, although its scenery is not at all inferior to that in the vicinity of Zahleh, Zibdâny, Djezzin, or Deir-el-Kamr. Frequent excursions can be made from Beyrout to every part of the mountain, but there is one excursion—to Ghazir, Harîsa, and Antoura in the Kesrawân—which will be found of especial interest. I remained only one night at each of these places, but I should advise any person that may follow the route indicated in the present chapter, to spend, at least, an entire day at Ghazir and Beit-Cash-Bow, as well as at Harîsa and Antoura, thus extending the excursion to eight days instead of four.

It would take months to travel over the Lebanon, to stop at all its lovely sites, and visit all its romantic villages. It is everywhere mountainous, it is true, but some variety or some new feature is always presenting itself. I know of nothing more curative in its effect, or more likely to benefit the health of a dyspeptic invalid, than a residence at Beyrout, and an occasional ride over those beautiful hills. It is well known, as I have already said, that impressions made upon the mind are influenced materially by the condition of the body, and the one constantly reacts upon the other. It is proverbial that the objective world takes the tone and tinge of our mind—that the sun has no brightness and the flower no beauty for the unhappy; while if the heart is light, hope sanguine, and our prospects brilliant, the deepest gloom of a winter's night cannot sadden us. Every one of any sensibility must have experienced this, and we have well-known illustrations of the fact in such instances as the imbecile torpor into which the great Chatham fell when the hereditary malady that had so long racked his body seemed to retire inwards, and paralyze his mind—when he retired to Hayes and could not even hear business mentioned without an attack of the nerves; in the anecdote about Ravaillac, or some other regicide, who declared that, if he had taken the cooling medicine he required, he should not have attempted the king's life: so true it is that

> "Infirmity doth still neglect all office
> Whereto our health is bound ; we are not ourselves
> When nature, being oppressed, commands the mind
> To suffer with the body."

No doubt the tone and state of the mind are often the result, not merely of the condition of our physical organism, but of external influence and circumstances. There is a continual reciprocal action going on between the outer world and our mind and feelings. Now, in Syria, the climate and scenery have all the elements for restoring any derangement of our corporeal functions. Skies ever sunny and serene; an atmosphere pure, translucid, and exhilarating; the entire aspect of nature combining the elements of the grand and the beautiful; the impressions produced by mountains towering to the skies, and landscapes replete with gentle loveliness;—all impress, with their various and cheering characteristics, the minds of those who are within their influence.

The traveller over those mountains feels a buoyancy that seems, as it were, to lift him from the earth; and turn which way he will, there are objects admirably adapted to soothe and charm the senses, to excite and ravish the imagination. No wonder, then, that he should be free alike from indigestion and low spirits, from lassitude and *ennui;* that the joyous brightness and beauty without, should light up a cheerful serenity within; that his mind should be in the healthiest and happiest state for receiving the gayest and most pleasing impressions, and that these should fix themselves in his memory, and be ever after recurred to with delight.

I have good reason to remember my first excursion to Mount Lebanon. Previous to visiting Syria, I had been for two years in the "doctors' hands," and many persons, unhappily, know what that means. A sedentary occupation and overwork had produced dyspepsia of a severe character, which the prescriptions of several "eminent" medical men only tended to intensify and confirm. The voyage from Marseilles *viâ* Alexandria to Beyrout was of considerable benefit; at the expiration of a month in Beyrout, I re-commenced to enjoy existence, and this first excursion to Mount Lebanon was the turning-point in that complete restoration to health which I have since enjoyed.

When travelling in Syria, it is always advisable to start on a journey before daybreak, so as to be able to rest during the heat of the mid-day sun. This precaution is specially necessary when riding over the plains, although not of the same importance on the mountains. The sun had not risen when we quitted our hotel, and walked through the deserted bazaars to the Grande Place, where we mounted our horses. In about a quarter of an hour we passed the spot where, it is said, St. George slew the dragon.* A little

---

* Some persons are so sceptical as to disbelieve the story relative to this terrible dragon, whose daily meal was a youthful virgin sent from Beyrout; until, at length, the beautiful princess, on whom the lot had fallen, was fortunately rescued by St. George. These unbelievers even assert that the marks shown on the wall, near the cave, are not the marks left by the Saint when he washed his hands after the combat, but merely stains left by the hand of Time. It is, however, undoubted that St. George was a Knight of Cappadocia, of good family, and suffered martyrdom during the reign of Diocletian, A.D. 290. It has been stated that the Saint was held in great estimation among the English even in the Saxon period; but I am inclined to assign the reign of Henry II. as the epoch when we became intimately acquainted with the hero, as he was then raised to the rank of first tutelar saint in the calendar, upon the marriage of

further on, we crossed the old Roman bridge over the Nahr-Beyrout, and a canter of an hour and a half on the Mediterranean shore brought us to the Nahr-el-Kelb, or Dog River, where we refreshed our horses, and then pushed on to Junêh, which we reached in about forty minutes. The village of Junêh is a favourite resort of the Beyroutines during the bathing season. The houses are built in the form of an amphitheatre on the side of a hill, facing the sea,—terrace above terrace, to a considerable height, affording from each the most exquisite views of water, plain, and mountain. We breakfasted in a charming little cottage overlooking the bay, and, after a couple of hours' rest, commenced the ascent to Ghazir.

There is no actual road from Junêh to Ghazir, but the difficulties of the journey are amply repaid by the magnificent scenery met with in ascending the mountain. On the slopes and acclivities, tufts of shrubs and clumps of trees assume the most picturesque and even fantastic forms; some growing in the shape of a cone, others spreading out like an umbrella, or forming

Henry with Eleanor, daughter of William of Aquitaine, who died fighting for the Holy Sepulchre, and whose patron saint was St. George.

a thick tangled mass of luxuriant foliage, like a colossal bush. Every variety of tint, shape, and size of leaf, too, is to be seen; a vast variegated labyrinth where the deep hue of the orange, the bright yellow of the lemon, the dark colour of the cypress, the leaden green of the delicate leaf of the mulberry, the beautiful pomegranate, innumerable parasitic plants hanging from over-arching branches,—all mingle in a thousand wild and charming combinations, as novel as they are lovely. The ground itself is a soft carpet of greensward strewn with the brightest flowers; while, here and there, plots of barley wave and bend to the breeze, or the spreading caroub covers the sylvan homestead of a peasant, with its garden full of brilliant-coloured plants, and its porch shaded by a clustering vine, under which you are invited to take rest and shelter. Milk, with bread and fruit, is offered to you, and a nosegay, at parting, testifies the good-will of the humble but hospitable little household. Continuing to ascend the mountain, the horizon beyond the plain seems to recede and widen, while the terraces left behind have a charming effect, which I can compare to nothing so much as a brilliant cloth or tissue of many colours, all blended and arranged so as to present a sort of symmetrical disorder; a wild spontaneous harmonizing of vegetable forms, the beauty of which, without being seen, it is almost impossible to realize.

Two hours' ride up the mountain from Junêh brought us to the monastery of Beit-Cash-Bow, where we received a cordial welcome from the Armenian fathers. An excellent dinner, served in European style, with wines of Mount Lebanon and France, was in due time placed before us, and, after a pleasant chat over our pipes and coffee, I retired to a comfortable bed, and slept more soundly than I had done for years. The next morning, Sunday, we had an excellent opportunity of seeing the Maronites in their fine church, and, afterwards, walked across the hills to the Jesuit college at Ghazir. Our guide was the village doctor, but his professional emoluments, I fancy, were very trifling, as he willingly accepted six piastres (one shilling) at parting.

Returning to the monastery, we encountered a Maronite princess, attended by her maidens,—forming one of the prettiest living pictures I had ever seen. The princess's dress consisted of a blue silk pelisse, fringed with gold cord, over a pink silk vest embroidered in gold; a rich shawl bound round her waist, loose trousers of yellow silk, and yellow leather papooshes. Her face was concealed by a white veil, which hung from the tantoor,* but, as we stood admiringly, she withdrew the veil for a moment to take a look at the *frangi*, disclosing a complexion exceedingly fair, and a face of perfect beauty. The dresses of her maidens, although less rich, were scarcely less picturesque. The costumes of the men were also very brilliant, consisting of a short red or blue embroidered cloth jacket over a gay-coloured silk vest; a rich scarf round the waist, containing silver-inlaid pistols or ivory-hafted daggers; loose trousers fastened over the shoe by embroidered gaiters; and the head-dress of the country—the red tarbûsh.

The road to Harîza discloses beauties of a different nature from those seen in the ascent from Junêh to Ghazir; more wild and grand, yet revealing, here and there, some charming spots

* The tantoor is a conical tube of silver, from a foot to two feet in length, and about three inches in width at the bottom, and one inch at the top. It is secured to a pad on the head by two silken cords, which hang down the back, and terminate in large tassels or knobs of silver. The narrow end projects over the forehead at an angle of 45 degrees, and supports a long white veil that falls gracefully round the shoulders, and, when required, covers the face. The tantoor is worn only by married women.

of surpassing loveliness. It seems like an effort of nature to group into one great maze the most diversified and opposite characteristics of oriental scenery. Every emotion of our æsthetic faculties—our sentiment of the beautiful, our conception of the sublime—are here all called forth together, and arise in the mind at once. For hours over these heights, the place of destination is continually in sight, yet seems to recede as you approach; or, as we read in fairy tales, as if your horse seemed to move, or your feet perform the function of walking, without any progress, or one step in advance having been made. Distance, seen across the vast expanse of open valley and through the clear transparent atmosphere, is almost inappreciable. We know that the inexperienced eye of a person confined in a cell from birth would take no cognizance of perspective, and see nothing in the finest landscape but a variously coloured surface. It is only when the sense of sight is rectified by the other senses, and confirmed by judgment—unconsciously, it may be, and without our taking notice of it at the time—that we are able to judge of distances. Thus, on visiting the Highlands of Scotland for the first time, the mighty masses of mountain and open sweep of moor and water make a stronger impression upon a stranger than on a person who has been accustomed to range over the hills, and whose eyes have become familiar with the prospect. The stranger is not so well able to judge of distance and relative size, because he finds himself amidst scenery that is new to him; and his power of appreciating perspective, acquired from the top of Primrose Hill or the heights of Gravesend, altogether fails. From a little hillock called Belmont, at Stanmore, and also from Brockley Hill, on the St. Albans Road, the Crystal Palace at Sydenham can be seen, when the day is sufficiently clear—which, however, seldom happens—and it is difficult to believe that the edifice is at the distance we know it to be. On Mount Lebanon, this effect is heightened by the extreme clearness and transparency of the atmosphere, places seen over vast tracts of valley seem close at hand, when, in fact, they are many hours' journey off. The traveller is thus often out in his reckoning; but even when deceived, he is not disappointed, for he certainly would not surrender a step of the way,—leading as it does through a natural garden, where the spontaneous efforts of nature surpass all that art has ever accomplished.

Sometimes the path lies along the course of a

torrent, the bed of which has been dried up by the summer heats. On either hand, rocks, to the height of four hundred feet, rise like perpendicular walls. Gigantic blocks and boulder-like masses lie scattered irregularly in every variety of position, as if shot down and strewn about the surface at random. Some rest on their broadest side, firm and solid as a pyramid, and seem destined to remain fixed for ages; while others sit, fantastically, upon their apex, with such apparent instability that they appear as if a child could push them over. On emerging from these rugged gorges, you come out, from time to time, into some shady highland valley,—a little paradise of verdure; while, here and there, green flights of stairs lead up to eminences, like the steps of some vast altar erected to nature in one of her most favourite haunts.

Villages appear perched, like birds' nests, on ledges of the cliff, or seem to hang upon the mountain's shelving side. Two of these villages will be so close together that a stone may be thrown from one to the other, yet a deep chasm intervenes, the path round which it will take a long time to traverse. Ascending still higher up the mountain, more extensive views of sea and plain are obtained. Spread out, too, as in a maze, are wooded knolls and grassy valleys; waterfalls glittering in silver showers and bounding in spray from rock to rock. In one direction, perhaps, a wreath of mist envelops the landscape; while in another you see the welcome turrets of a monastery through the trees, and your attention is arrested by the rude harmony of the shepherd's pipe and the tinkling of the sheep-bells. Suddenly, the path seems brought to an end by a craggy ledge of rock, the side of which goes sheer down for some hundreds of feet; but the guide points out a narrow winding way between rugged masses, where the utmost caution is necessary, as a single careless step might send you headlong into an abyss so deep that escape, with life, would be impossible.

On these occasions, it is prudent to leave mules and horses to their own judgment and discretion, and, when not tampered with, they are rarely known to stumble. It is usual to account for their surefootedness by saying, "It is instinct;" but this explanation is about as intelligible as that of the doctor in the French comedy, who, being asked why laudanum put people to sleep, replied, "Because it possesses a soporific quality." It is curious to see how the animals examine the path they are traversing, and how careful they are in making good their foremost foothold on the rock, before moving another step in advance. It would indeed seem as if their mode of acquiring experience was very much the same as our own. The sagacity of the Arabian horses, and their almost human qualities, have become proverbial, but their extraordinary degree of polish, so to speak, arises from their constantly sharing the society of their masters, and from the education—for it is an education—which they receive. They may be said to eat, drink, and sleep with their owners—are their companions at home and abroad, share their habitations, and carry them with speed over the desert sands, into which an English horse would sink nearly to his knees. The colt always attends its dam, runs by her side when on a journey, and shares the caresses of her master and his family. By thus following the actions of its mother over the treacherous footing of the desert or the precipitous paths up the mountain, it acquires, almost without artificial training, a degree of sagacity and dexterity that is almost incredible. During my residence in Syria, I possessed an Arab horse that carried me everywhere. He was wild like his race, and yet, with me, as gentle as a lamb. At the slightest motion of my hand, he would fly like the wind, or stop in an instant. When tired, we have lain down together, my head pillowed on his shoulder. He would follow me like a dog, and stand perfectly quiet for me to mount, yet it was a most dangerous feat for any one else to try to get into the saddle. When leaving Beyrout, I parted from many friends, but from none with greater regret than from my horse, Duroc.

Eight hours' ride from Ghazîr brought us to the monastery of Harîsa, where we received even a more hearty welcome than that at Beit-Cash-Bow. We dined with the brothers in the refectory, and the repast, though not so varied as the one of which we partook on the day previous, was exceedingly good; the hospitable Prior producing, for our special consumption, some exquisite old Lebanon wine, which, he said, had lain in the cellar for a number of years. Lebanon wine, I may mention, is, when fully matured, equal in flavour to the finest East India Madeira.

Early next morning, we started on our journey from Harîsa; some new beauty in the scenery displaying itself at every step, until in the midst of a site teeming with a luxuriant flora—the mulberry, the fig, the orange, the sycamore, and the pine—the charming village of Antoura lay in a valley before us. At each turn in the descent, its wonderful fertility and profuse vegetation, its picturesque position, surrounded with lofty mountains, astonished and delighted us, and the exclamation of the Eastern poet came to my lips: "If there be a paradise on earth, it is this—it is this!"

We were courteously received by the superior of the Lazarist college, and shown over the school-rooms, dormitories, dining-hall, and playgrounds. The pupils to the number of three hundred come from Beyrout, Aleppo, Damascus, and other towns in Syria, Persia, Egypt, and even from Nubia and Abyssinia. They are boarded, lodged, and educated for fifteen hundred piastres (about £12 10s.) per annum; or including all extras, with the exception of clothes, for two thousand piastres (about £16 13s. 4d.); and are taught the French, Italian, Latin, Greek, and Arabic languages; writing, arithmetic, and the usual branches of an European education. We dined with the boys, at the professor's table, and found the food excellent. The following morning I had a delicious breakfast, as, on opening my bed-room window, I found the golden fruit of an orange-tree hanging like bunches of grapes within my reach.

It added much to the picturesqueness of the scene, as we rode over the hills on leaving Antoura, to meet some of the pupils returning after vacation, mounted on horses or mules, and followed by camels bearing their brightly-painted boxes. As the boys passed, they all saluted after the manner of the country,—a form of salutation which is much more graceful than that prevailing in many other countries. At New Guinea, the mode is certainly picturesque; for the people place leaves of trees upon their hands as symbols of peace and friendship. An Ethiopian takes the robe of another and ties it round his own waist, leaving his friend partially naked—a custom which in a cold climate would not be very agreeable. Sometimes it is usual, as a sign of humility, for persons to place themselves naked before those whom they salute;—as when Sir Joseph Banks received the visit of two Otaheitan females. The inhabitants of the Philippine Islands take the hand or foot of him they salute, and gently rub their face with it—a proceeding which is, at all events, more agreeable than that prevailing with the Laplanders, who have a habit of rubbing noses, applying their own with some degree of force to that of the person they desire to honour. The salute with which you are greeted in Syria is at once graceful and flattering. The hand is raised, with a quick but gentle motion, to the heart, the lips, and the forehead; thus intimating that the person who salutes is willing to think, speak, and act for you.

At a distance of about an hour from Antoura, we rested at the convent of Deir-Beshâra, where sweetmeats, confections, and mountain wine were cheerfully placed before us. The nuns could only speak Arabic; but, from their retreat behind a screen, they conversed for some time by means of an interpreter. Passing through the little village of Zook, where the superb gold and silver brocades, sold in the bazaars of Beyrout, are manufactured, we soon arrived at the Nahr-el-Kelb, and rested under the pleasant shade of the "Hôtel Pittoresque." Here, after a little time, we partook of a simple repast, consisting of fish, caught in the river after our arrival, pilaff, and fowl. Figs from Smyrna, pistachios from Aleppo, oranges from Jaffa, and apricots from Damascus, formed our desert, with wines of Cyprus and Lebanon cooled in pressed snow from the peaks of Jebel-Sunnîn. Before we rose to depart, the sun had disappeared below the horizon, and, as there is little or no twilight in Syria, the shades of night suddenly closed around, wrapping mountain, sea, and river in the deepest gloom. The moon, however, was near the full, and soon began to brighten up the landscape; its soft and gentle light presenting a marked contrast to the fiery glow of the sun, and displaying a wonderful scene of loveliness and grandeur. On every object—in the sky, on the dark frowning masses of the mountain, in the broad and shining bosom of the sea—was written, "Behold the Eternal." The very air breathed the spirit of devotion—the earth and the heavens seemed instinct with the power and presence of the Omnipotent, unseen yet felt.

We sent our horses home by the shore, and returned by water. The sea was perfectly calm; the Arab boatmen sang their favourite songs, and a pleasant row of an hour and a half brought us to Beyrout.

CHAPTER VI.

BEYROUT TO JERUSALEM AND DAMASCUS.

An excursion to Jerusalem can very easily be made from Beyrout.* The Austrian Lloyd's and French steamers leave frequently during each week, arriving the following morning at Jaffa, where there is an hotel — Howard's Hotel — pleasantly situated near the sea. The position of Jaffa is very fine, and the port, the southernmost in Syria, is the *entrepôt* for Jerusalem, Nablous, Gaza, and the interior of this part of the country. To it is brought the whole surplus produce of the valley of the Jordan for shipment, and, as cultivation is largely on the increase, Jaffa will probably become a very important emporium of trade. A railway from Jaffa to Jerusalem would be a great boon to travellers, as, at present, the only wheeled

---

* I purposely omit any description of Jerusalem or Damascus. The tourist can consult his "Murray's Hand-Book."

conveyance is a small omnibus that performs the journey, three times a week, in about fourteen hours. It is more preferable, however, to hire horses at Jaffa, as the ride over the flowery plains of Sharon should not be omitted. Ramleh, the first station, is about four hours from Jaffa, and the traveller can there obtain refreshment and rest for the night with the hospitable monks of the Latin convent. From Ramleh, excursions can be made to Esdouad, the Ashdod of Samuel, where Dagon fell before the ark; Azotus, where Philip was found after baptizing the eunuch; Gath, the town of Goliath; and Ludd, the Lydda of the Acts. Starting in the early morning, *en route* from Ramleh, you reach the valley of Ajalon in about three hours, and three hours and a half more bring you to Kirjath-Jearim, or "City of the Woods," where, it is said, the ark rested for twenty years. At a little distance is the valley of Elah; at two hours, Emmaus; and then, about twenty miles farther, is seen the Holy City of Jerusalem. There are now two very good hotels in Jerusalem: the "Damascus Hotel," near the Holy Sepulchre; and the "Mediterranean Hotel," near the British Consulate. Four days will suffice to see the principal objects of interest in the city, and excursions can be made, at leisure, to Bethany, Jericho, the Jordan and Dead Sea, Solomon's pools, and Hebron; returning to Beyrout *viâ* Jaffa.

The excursion to Damascus will be found very pleasant, as there is now an excellent road between that city and Beyrout. The making of this fine carriage road, a distance of about seventy miles, has been of the greatest benefit, not only to its terminal cities, but to the whole district through which it runs. Viewed as a specimen of civil engineering, the work is highly creditable; the road being carried across the range of the Lebanon and Anti-Lebanon, by easy gradients, at the respective elevations of 6000 and 4000 feet, and at a cost which makes the working of the road a highly remunerative business to the shareholders. The company have the monopoly of all wheeled conveyances over the road for a term of fifty years; and the traveller between Beyrout and Damascus is now able to engage a seat in a well-appointed diligence—the time occupied being only twelve to fourteen hours—while the merchant can send his goods in the company's covered waggons without entertaining a doubt as to their due arrival in good order and condition. It is a rather curious coincidence that this road company, under

French direction, should be a great commercial success, while the Beyrout Water-Works Company, under English direction, has turned out an utter failure. Demetri's Hotel at Damascus is, next to Missirie's at Constantinople, the most comfortable hotel in the East, and provides every accommodation that can be reasonably desired. Two days, at least, should be devoted to visit the bazaars, khans, baths, mosques, churches, and other sights of this ancient city, which is said to be the oldest in the world.

CHAPTER VII.

BEYROUT TO NAZARETH.

THE route indicated in the present chapter is out of the ordinary track of tourists, and will serve to show the facility with which excursions can be made from Beyrout.

Leaving Beyrout by the Austrian Lloyd's steamer, at 10 o'clock P.M. on Friday, we landed next morning, after a pleasant passage of eight hours, at Kaiffa, the ancient Sycaminum of the Romans, beautifully situated at the foot of Mount Carmel. Here, my excellent friend, Her Majesty's Vice-Consul, gave us a hearty welcome, and, after breakfast, we mounted our horses, and started, at one o'clock, *en route* for Nazareth. The road from Kaiffa winds, for some time, through fields and gardens to the village of Belled-esh-Sheikh, which is reached in about an hour. Half an hour thence is the village of Yahoor, near the river Kishon, which we forded, and an hour and a half more brought us to El-Hartîe, about midway between Kaiffa and Nazareth. Leaving El-Hartîe, we entered a forest of dwarf oaks intermingled with trees bearing white blossoms like the orange; the ground being one carpet of flowers, in which the anemone was most conspicuous. It was a delightful spot—

"A seat where gods might dwell,
And wander with delight."

Passing through this forest, we came in sight of the plains of Esdraelon and the mountains of Gilboa. In an hour from El-Hartîe, we rode at a canter through the village of Jeidâh, and half an hour more brought us to the spring of Semûnieh—the Simonias of Josephus.* As we reclined to rest ourselves here, several women approached to draw water at the spring, clad in their picturesque costume, and appearing in every respect as in the time of Christ. Nearly two thousand years have passed, and the dress, habits, and customs of the people remain unchanged.

Many of the wandering Bedawîns, armed to

---

* It was in this place that the Romans attempted during the night to seize Josephus.

the teeth, looked very formidable as they passed on their fleet horses, but we greeted them with civility; and here I may remark that I have never, in any part of Palestine or Syria, received aught but courtesy and respect from the natives. If they are treated kindly, they will be respectful; but many travellers think it necessary to assert a claim to superiority, and, in some instances, suffer in consequence. In another hour and a half—six hours altogether from Kaiffa—we rode down the steep hills that encompass Nazareth, and alighted at the hospitable dwelling of the monks of Terra Santa. The sun had set; night had quickly succeeded day, and the town looked picturesque as the lights twinkled in the darkness. The heart quivered, and awe crept over the frame, for, here, we stood on holy ground. On this very spot, perhaps, our feet trod in the footsteps of Christ, for here His youth was passed, and over these hills He wandered.

The next day, Sunday, we visited the Church of the Annunciation—second only to that of the Holy Sepulchre—the Greek Church, the Well of the Virgin, the Mensa Christi, the presidents of the Greek and Latin communities, &c. On Monday, as the rain—the "latter rain" of Scripture — prevented our going to Tiberias, we paid a visit to the superior of the Church of the Annunciation, who received us with every courtesy, and, after coffee, sent one of the brothers to conduct us over the chapel built on the site of St. Joseph's workshop. Above the altar, in this chapel, there is a most exquisite painting. In the centre stands Joseph in his workshop, holding the handle of a carpenter's axe, the edge of which rests on a block of wood; his eyes are directed, with a mingled expression of affection and reverence, towards the child Jesus, who, with a book in his hand, the contents of which he is evidently expounding, sits on a low stool in the foreground. On the left sits the Virgin, eagerly listening to her son, and casting upon him looks of tenderness and love. It was a picture of home, and recalled in full force to my imagination the early scenes of our Saviour's life. In that very room where I stood, our Lord had sat, and talked, and was obedient unto his parents. There He assisted Joseph; there He grew up to manhood ere He went forth on that saving mission which ended with his death. In and about Jerusalem, the remembrances are sad and gloomy, but at Nazareth, they tell of happiness and peace. I could not soon tear myself from the place made sacred by these associations, and I do not envy the man who could stand there unmoved. I plucked a wild flower from the garden trodden by our Saviour's steps,—a mute memento of the hallowed spot.

The clouds which had hung over the valley during the morning being now dispersed, we rode to the hill that, from the west, overlooks Nazareth, and on which stands the lonely wely, or tomb, of Neby Ismael. There is a glorious prospect from the summit of this hill, and the air is deliciously pure and fresh. The western part of the great plain of Esdraelon stretched out at our feet. To the left, Mount Tabor towered above the intervening hills. On the west Gilboa and Hermon, and the mountains of Samaria stretching from Jenîn to the chain that extends from Carmel. Mount Carmel itself, with the town of Kaiffa on the shore beneath, and the town of Acre, washed by the Mediterranean, on the shore beyond. To the north, extends one of the vast plains of Palestine, called El-Bûttauf, which yields a tributary stream to the Kishon. To the south, can be seen a large village on the side of the hill, the ancient Sepphoris, now called Seffûrich. Beyond the plain of El-Bûttauf, extend long ridges of hills running east and west, and, in the extreme distance, stands Safed, "the city set upon a hill." To the right, there is a curious grouping of hills and mountains, above which a still loftier chain rises in the distance far away.

Most persons have probably felt, at some time or other, how much the pleasure derived from scenery is enhanced by certain familiar reminiscences, and how much more attractive nature appears when associated with the remembrance of some dear friend, or the forms of those we loved. If such be the case, what pleasure must be felt in the contemplation of scenes like these, where every spot is hallowed by recollections dear to our hearts, and where, at every step, remembrances of Him who loved us appeal so strongly to our imagination. Every place near Nazareth is, in fact, full of interest, but the road to Tiberias is, perhaps, more so than any other. Passing by Kefr-Kenna, the Cana of Galilee—where the house is shown in which the miracle was performed of turning water into wine—we come to the Mount of Beatitudes. Further on is the scene of the miracle of the loaves and fishes, and then before us is Lake Gennesareth. There is little in Tiberias itself worthy of observation, if we except the church, which is said to have been built on the spot where stood the house of Peter.

It is the associations in the mind that invest everything around with interest, for although doubts may be cast on many traditional sites, there is no doubt that on these waters our Lord walked in the stillness of the night; on these waters the tempest-tossed ship of the disciples laboured amidst the storm.* At Tiberias, there is little or no accommodation for travellers. The best way, therefore, to visit Gennesareth is to leave Nazareth at daybreak, going north-east over the hills to Er-Reineh, a small village half an hour distant, and thence to Kefr-Kenna;

* In the Church of the Annunciation, I asked the brother who attended us if he were certain that the grotto under the altar was really the place where the Angel Gabriel saluted the Virgin, and he replied, "I really cannot be certain, for I do not know of my own knowledge; but when I find that it and several similar places have, from the earliest days of Christianity, been pointed out and held sacred; when I find that in those early days, piety, in order to commemorate and hand them down to posterity, erected costly churches over them; and when these have been destroyed by the enemies of our faith, the piety of succeeding ages has again restored them,—I see no reason to doubt the truth of the traditions thus so clearly marked and handed down to us."

then passing the village of El-Meshad, situated on a high hill to the left, and so by Lûbieh to Tiberias;—returning the same afternoon in time to reach the summit of Mount Tabor, and behold the magnificent view and glorious sunset. When I visited Mount Tabor, a solitary hermit had made his home on the summit. He had lived in the Crimea; but, having dreamt that he should pass the remainder of his life in prayer and meditation upon a mountain in Palestine, he made a pilgrimage to the Holy Land, and wandered till he came in sight of Mount Tabor, which corresponded exactly in appearance with the mountain he had seen in his dream. After some time, he discovered the ruins of the Church of the Transfiguration, which had been destroyed in A.D. 1263, by the Sultan Bibars. He excavated until he reached several chambers, some of which he roofed in and occupied. From Mount Tabor to Nazareth is a ride of an hour and a half.

The attention and hospitality of the monks of Terra Santa, during our visit, could not be exceeded. The bed-rooms in the monastery were neat and clean, and the fare placed before us was excellent. We left Nazareth early on Wednesday morning, and, after an hour's ride, came to the fountain of Seffûrieh,* which was peaceably occupied by women washing clothes in the stream. The women of Nazareth and the neighbourhood do not veil their faces, but walk erect with a graceful and elegant carriage. They are tall and handsome, the profile being really beautiful, with that line of forehead and nose we see in the masterpieces of Ancient Greece. Their head-dress is peculiar. Instead of the gold or silver coins, worn in their long tresses by the women of Beyrout, the Nazarene women wear a multiplicity of coins—overlapping one another and attached to a pad on the head—so placed that they form a sort of frame, through which their faces appear as in a picture. Bracelets and silver anklets give a further addition to the picturesqueness of their costume. In half

---

* It was here, in A.D. 1187, that the flower of the Christian chivalry assembled, to the number of fifty thousand, before the fatal battle of Hattîn. Count Raymond, of Tripolis, advised that they should remain encamped near the fountain, and await Salah-ed-dîn; but the proud and impetuous Grand Templar prevailed upon the weak king, Guy de Lusignan, to march towards Tiberias, and the result was a final blow to the power of the Crusaders. A few days after the battle of Hattîn, the victorious Salah-ed-dîn encamped at the fountain, whence he continued his triumphant march to Acre.

an hour from the fountain, we reached the village of Seffûrich—the Sepphoris of Josephus and Diocæsarea of the Romans—which, in the time of Herod Antipater, was the largest and strongest city of Galilee. Leaving the ruins of the church, built on the site of Joachim and Anna's house, to the right, we shortly entered the flowery plain of Zabulon, and, ascending the hills near Shefâ-Omar, came in view of the Mediterranean and the town of Acre. Crossing these hills, we descended into the plain of Abilîn, and, on reaching the heights above the village—four hours from Nazareth— we unexpectedly came upon an encampment of Bedawîns under the command of Salihl Aga, by whom we were most hospitably received.

CHAPTER VIII.

A DAY WITH THE BEDAWÎNS.

I HAVE seldom beheld a more animated or picturesque scene than that which presented itself as we suddenly halted on the hill overlooking the village of Abilîn. The dark tents of the Hawâras dotted the hill sides, and stretched far away into the plain beyond. Crowds of handsome, though rather wild-looking men— some reclining under the tents, others sauntering up and down, or placidly smoking their chibouks; while, apart, on a rich Persian carpet, sat Salihl-Aga, chief of the tribe, surrounded by his principal officers, numerous secretaries, with silver ink-holders stuck like daggers in their scarfs, and several distinguished-looking Arabs, who, I subsequently learned, were relatives and guests. As we hesitated to advance, Salihl-Aga at once sent his first lieutenant to beg us to alight, and, almost at the same moment, our horses were taken possession of by the grooms, while we willingly obeyed the chief's request. As I approached, Salihl-Aga and his officers arose; the latter giving place to me on the right hand of their chief, whose graceful salutation I returned by bending low, and placing my hand on my heart, my lips, and my forehead. Taking our seats on the carpets spread upon the ground, Salihl-Aga and I repeated our salutation, and, then, according to Oriental etiquette, I saluted each officer in due form, one after the other, beginning with the one nearest to me, every man responding by a bow, and laying his hand on his mouth and forehead. Two Nubians then approached with two nargilehs exactly alike, and presented them, at identically the same instant, to me and the chief, who bowed, as if he would render to me the homage due to a superior.* Coffee was then brought to us in china and silver filigree cups, the same ceremony being observed

* In the East, paradoxical as it may appear, the guest is, for the moment, the host. When a Syrian—Mussulman or Christian—receives you into his house, he, for the time, ceases to be master. He places himself, his servants, and his house at your disposal, and, while he supplies all your wants, he appears rather as the guest, and you as the host and superior.

as with the nargilehs—the chief and I emptying our cups and returning them simultaneously to the attendants, so as to make our salutations at the same time. Coffee was afterwards handed to the officers, who, as they returned the cups, again saluted; and, the strictness of etiquette being apparently relaxed, conversation became general. Salihl-Aga then informed us that they were celebrating the wedding of his son, Mohammed Ali, with the daughter of his brother, Akili-Aga; the bridegroom having attained his eighteenth year, and the bride having seen fourteen summers.

After a little time, servants approached with silver jugs containing cold water, which they poured over our hands, while other domestics presented fine napkins richly embroidered in gold. This ceremony completed, a huge dish of boiled rice, with a boiled lamb on the top, was placed before us. Leben, or sour goats' milk, was poured here and there into the rice, a small quantity of which was taken up in the palm of the hand, rolled into the form and size of a pigeon's egg, and then transferred to the mouth. We had neither knives nor forks;—the lamb being torn and eaten with the fingers. I enjoyed this breakfast immensely. The rice was well boiled; the lamb tender; the tail delicious; and having ridden during four hours in the pure morning air, I was decidedly hungry. At first, I was rather shy of the tail; but the chief lieutenant tore a piece off and presented it to me—an act of special courtesy,—and it was really excellent. To Europeans, this eating with the fingers seems unpleasant, but the ablutions so scrupulously performed, before and after meals, prevent any idea of uncleanliness. After breakfast, native musicians and dancers— the latter being dressed as women—appeared upon the scene. The performance, although novel and graceful, was rather sensuous, and I was not sorry when Salihl-Aga gave the signal to mount our horses, and proceed to the more stirring business of the day.

The chief, at the head of about five hundred horsemen, now led the way down a hill to a plain of considerable extent, where an opposing force of similar strength was drawn up under the command of his son, Mohammed Ali. The women and children assembled on the heights, and the combatants, as they faced each other, looked as if they had met to decide the fate of Abilîn. For some moments not a man moved. At length, Salihl-Aga advanced leisurely and alone towards the ranks of the enemy, and, brandishing his long spear almost in their faces, challenged them to the combat. Three of the enemy, one after the other, put spurs to their horses, and sprang forward to capture the challenger, who instantly wheeled, then turned suddenly, again wheeling, and leaning so low over his horse's neck, to evade the enemy's blow, as to be for a moment lost to sight; then rising and reining in his splendid Arab, he discharged his pistols at the foe as they passed in their headlong speed. Pursued again, he turned once more, and, throwing the reins on his horse's neck, unslung his carbine, discharging it in the face of his would-be captor as he advanced upon him; then, seizing the reins, guided his horse at full speed into the ranks of his own men, who, in their turn, advanced to the attack, and charged the enemy up to the opposite line. Thus, in a short time, the entire forces on both sides were engaged, and the whole field became the scene of a great battle, in which the eye followed the two principal figures—the chiefs of the contending hosts. The young bridegroom exhibited wonderful skill in eluding the attacks of his pursuers; wheeling in an instant on his nearest foe, the bridle thrown carelessly on the neck of his steed, while he unslung his carbine, which in a real contest would have brought down many an antagonist. Salihl-Aga himself, in the excitement of the fight, let fall his turban and gold-embroidered cloak,—exhibiting his shaven crown, with one long plait of hair floating in the wind; and, as he led on a charge, uttering his shrill war-cry, it was difficult to fancy the combat otherwise than real. The prancing and excited horses; the brilliant and various costumes of the combatants; the white burnouses streaming in the air; the clatter of steel and silver housings; the shouts of the men, and loud reports of pistol and musket; the chivalric bearing of Salihl-Aga, and the noble mien of Mohammed Ali; the women and children on the heights between the village and the plain;—all made up a scene more wild and exciting than any I had ever before beheld.

The sham-fight over, the sport of casting the djerreed commenced, the activity required in which exceeds even that with the spear and pistol. Each horseman singles out an adversary, against whom he hurls his djerreed with considerable force, the skill consisting in catching it at the critical moment, and flinging it back again before the attacking party can escape.

This sport is not unattended with danger, as a well-directed blow from a djerreed has frequently been fatal. Sometimes, when it is found impossible to catch the djerreed, the Bedawy almost throws himself from the saddle, and, holding on to his horse's neck, lets the weapon pass over him; then, swiftly wheeling, pulls the djerreed from the ground, and hurls it at his retreating antagonist. The horse performs a conspicuous part in this tourney, as upon his sagacity and perfect training depend much of his rider's success.

The bridegroom, having now proved his valour, returned in triumph to the village. Most of his men had dismounted and followed on foot with drawn swords, two of the principal officers walking at either side of his horse;—their swords crossing over the animal's shoulders. Mohammed Ali held a bouquet in his right hand—a love-token which, according to Bedawîn custom, he must bring back to his bride, otherwise the marriage could not be consummated. Instances have occurred where a rival has attacked the bridegroom and carried off the love-token, and as its possessor can claim the bride, this part of the day's ceremony always possesses a special interest. As the *cortége* advanced, a band of men, armed with swords, rapidly descended the hill, while an equal number of the young chief's followers rushed to the front. For a second or two they stood facing each other, the bright steel glittering in the sun, and then the swords clashed,—beating time, with alternate strokes, to a strange wild dance, as they all proceeded towards the village. The crowd beat time with their hands, uttering shrill cries of heli-li-li-li-li-li-li, until the bridegroom alighted, and, being taken possession of by the women, disappeared from sight.

We bade farewell to our kind host, and, leaving Abilîn, entered the fertile plain of St. Jean d'Acre, through which a pleasant canter, over delightful green turf, brought us, in three hours, to the town itself, where we passed the night. The next day, Thursday, we inspected the fortifications, and then rode round the bay of Acre, about eight miles, to Mount Carmel, where we were hospitably received at the monastery of Elias,—the finest in the Holy Land. On Friday, at 8 A.M., we embarked at Kaiffa on board one of the Austrian Lloyd's steamers for Beyrout.

CHAPTER IX.

SYRIA.

When Greece was in her infancy, and long before Rome had even been founded, the coast of Syria was covered with magnificent and wealthy cities. On the north, stood Aradus (the modern Rouad); eighteen miles to the south, Tripolis; at a similar distance, Byblos (Djebeil), with the temple of Adonis; again further south, Berytus (Beyrout); at a like distance, Sidon; and, finally, about fifteen miles farther stood the "Queen of the Waters," the stately Tyre. From the latter city arose commerce, civilization, the arts and sciences, and, above all, that great instrument of social progress, the gift of letters. To its inhabitants, the Phœnicians, we are indebted for the knowledge of astronomy and arithmetic, as well as for the discovery of weights and measures, of money, of the art of keeping accounts, or book-keeping, for the invention, or at least for the improvement, of ship-building and navigation, and for the discovery of glass. They were also famous for the manufacture of fine linen and tapestry; for the art of working in metals and ivory; for their skill in architecture, and, especially, for the manufacture of that rare and costly luxury, the Tyrian purple.

A formidable rival, however, at length competed with Tyre, and the trade of the latter was, to some extent, transferred to Alexandria—that great city founded by the Macedonian conqueror. Nevertheless, Syria lost nothing of her material prosperity, for, when subsequently reduced to a Roman province (B.C. 65), the commerce which had created her wealth received an unexpected impulse, and found a new source of profit in the luxurious habits of her masters. Another and more remunerative market was immediately opened, as the conquerors, having once tasted the delights of Asia, soon felt wants unknown to their frugal forefathers, and eagerly demanded her perfumes, her silks, and her precious stones, which they paid for with the spoils of the world. The ports of Syria continued to send forth ships filled with rich and costly merchandise; with gold, silver, tin, and other metals; pearls, precious stones, and coral; mules, sheep, and goats; wheat, balm, oil, honey, spices, woven silk, and wine. Berytus (Beyrout) was famous for its immense exportation of corn, oil, and the choicest wines. The cedars of Lebanon furnished the Romans with wood for the domestic architecture of the rich, and the adornment of the temples of their gods. The dates of Syria were well known; for Galen, in one of his treatises, mentions their properties, and compares them with those of Egypt. The plums and other fruits of Damascus appeared, among various exotic luxuries, upon the tables of epicures; and Virgil tells us of a delicious species of pear, the cultivation of which had, in his time, been introduced from Syria into Italy.

After the fall of the Roman ascendancy (A.D. 638), this wondrous and classic land became the scene of many contests, and the battle-field on which the destinies of many dynasties were decided. Under the reign of the Khalifs, however, commerce again revived, and civilization made greater progress in two centuries than the world had ever seen before. The cities of Syria were re-embellished, an architecture of the highest order gave a charm to the buildings, and everything that human ingenuity could accomplish was effected for the welfare and prosperity of the country. History records the grandeur and magnificence of Haroun-al-Raschid, and the astonishment of Charlemagne at the presents sent to him by the Khalif; amongst which were perfumes, pearls, jewels, rich stuffs, arms, and a mechanical clock, worked by water, that then appeared to be a wonder in Europe. Haroun-al-Raschid, although he had to pay an army of five hundred thousand soldiers, and had built many palaces in different parts of his empire, was yet able to give his son, Al-Mamoun, two millions four hundred thousand denarii of gold; and when that prince was married, a thousand beautiful pearls were placed upon the head of his bride, and a lottery was opened in which each prize was either a house or a piece of land. Al-Mamoun was the Augustus of Islamism.

But all the glories of the Khalifs vanished before the hordes of Othman; and with the occupation of Syria by the Turks (A.D. 1517) set in a night of darkness, unrelieved, during more than three hundred years, by a single ray of light, or a single gleam of hope. This horde of Tartars, descending from the fastnesses of the Altäi range into the fair plains of Asia Minor and Syria, rushed like tigers upon their prey. They laid waste with fire and sword, destroying utterly whatever they could not appropriate; setting fire to whatever would burn, and razing to the ground whatever could be overturned. Statues, buildings, books, all shared in one common destruction. Every work of art and every useful contrivance, the appliances of science and the implements of trade, all disappeared together, like a crop of vegetation after a visit of locusts. They found a garden, but they made a desert!

There is an Arabic proverb which says that, "If a Turk could even excel in the knowledge of every science, barbarism would still remain inherent in his nature," and this is as true to-day as it was five hundred years ago. The habit, however, of using indifferently the words "Mussulman" and "Turk" has led to much misconception, as most persons imagine that "Mussulman" and "Turk" are synonymous terms, and, as a consequence, the whole Mussulman people are credited with the brutalities and the vices of their Turkish masters. On the contrary, the Mussulman possesses many natural virtues, and it is unfair to accuse him of the vices and crimes with which all classes of Turkish functionaries are justly charged. It is not Islamism, but the Turk, that is a bar to human progress.

When the Christian West was still sunk in comparative barbarism and ignorance, the Mussulman East was the home of civilization, of literature, of science, and of art. The Crusaders, it is well known, brought with them, on their return to Europe, the proofs of a civilization which, to them, had been hitherto unknown. The glories of Granada and the wonders of the Alhambra are written in the annals of Spain; and when Abou-Abdullah, commonly called Boabdil, stood in the pass of Apaxarras, and looked for the last time on the towers and spires of his lost capital, the most enlightened empire of that day passed away for ever. Chivalry had its root in Spain, whence Charlemagne transplanted it to the centre of Europe. The tournaments and jousts, the troubadours and knights-errant, Castilian pride, courtesy towards ladies, serenades, single combats, generosity towards the vanquished, faith in plighted word, respect for hospitality;— all were borrowed from the Mussulmans of

Spain. Even in the present day there is a great similarity between the Spanish character, in Andalusia, and that of the Arabs, who still possess many of the qualities which distinguished the warriors of Granada. I have sat under the tents of the Bedawîn, and partaken of their hospitality, and I can verify that there is not a finer or more naturally noble race in the universe. When I was in Syria, I could not avoid contrasting the physique of the Arab with that of the Turk, and I have often asked the former how it was that such a superior race should submit to the crushing rule of men who were, in every way, their inferiors. The answer was always the same: "We could live," they said, "in peace and amity with our Christian brethren, for we are all of the same land, and, if left to ourselves, would soon drive out the Turk. But we know that if we made the attempt, the fleet of England would soon be off our coast, and the soldiers of England be, perhaps, landed on our shores. Let the day come when we shall be free from foreign interference, and we—Mussulman and Christian together—will make short work with our Turkish masters."

The events which have recently taken place

in European Turkey continue to attract the attention of the civilized world towards the East. Some millions of human beings, crushed for centuries under the iron rule of the Turk, have at length been liberated; but the Osmanlis still dominate over that sacred region, endeared to the Arab and the Jew as the birthplace of their common Father Abraham, and to the Christian as the theatre of the Saviour's mission, and the scene of the Saviour's death. The civilization which had its birth in that land was driven away by rude and ignorant barbarians, and found a refuge in the West. What nobler task could the West now propose to itself than that of restoring civilization to its ancient home, and giving freedom to historic races that have for ages been oppressed? The energies of the people have, it is true, been kept down under the blighting *régime* of the Turk, but the land itself is as productive as of old, and, with the aid of Western science, Palestine and Syria might soon be restored to its ancient wealth and splendour. No country in the world could offer more favourable conditions to the immigrant for the enjoyment of a happy existence than the beautiful plains of Palestine and Syria, now lying untilled and fallow. Comparatively close to our own shores, they possess an exceptionally fertile soil, a salubrious climate, and are capable of producing in abundance every necessary for the wants of man.

For some years past, a considerable improvement in the commercial prosperity of Syria has been apparent; and if the traffic between Europe and India returns to its more direct course by the Mediterranean and Persian Gulf, this improvement will naturally continue. The royal cities of Nineveh and Babylon are, it is true, no more, and the mean towns of Mosul and Hillah alone mark the places where they stood; but the great rivers, the Tigris and the Euphrates, which contributed to their grandeur, are still capable of being made great arteries of trade. The Jordan, although only sixty feet wide, is, in some places twenty feet deep, and might easily be rendered navigable; while the Orontes rushes through the plain with a velocity that has induced the Arabs to call it El'-Asy, or the Rebel. The maritime cities of Syria are despoiled and neglected. Tyre, whose "merchants were princes, and her traffickers the honourable of the earth," has become "a place for the spreading of nets in the midst of the sea;" but the old Berytus still remains, bereft of her artificial splendour, yet possessing those natural beauties which time cannot destroy, and reviving, by her increasing trade, the memory of the vast commerce she once enjoyed, and the greatness to which, from her advantageous position, she is likely again to attain.

CHAPTER X.

THE BRITISH PROTECTORATE OF ASIATIC TURKEY.*

It has been said, on apparently good authority, that the aim which our Government hopes to carry out by virtue of the Anglo-Turkish Convention, is to establish the reign of justice within the Asiatic possessions of the Sultan. The task is a noble one, but the difficulties in the way of

---

* Few persons appear to understand the motives which have actuated Lord Beaconsfield in undertaking the Protectorate of Asiatic Turkey. Some thirty years ago, however, Mr. Disraeli visited the East, and in his book, "Tancred; or, The New Crusade," occurs the following passage:—" I'll tell you," said the Emir to Tancred, "the game is in our hands, if we have energy. There is a combination which would entirely change the whole face of the world, and bring back empire to the East. Though you are not the brother of the Queen of England, you are nevertheless a great English prince, and the Queen will listen to what you say; especially if you talk to her as you talk to me, and say such fine things in such a beautiful voice. Nobody ever opened my mind like you. You will magnetize the Queen as you have magnetized me. Go back to England and arrange this. Let

its accomplishment are so considerable that I am not surprised so many of our statesmen shrink from undertaking it. To regenerate Turkey in Asia is a work of which Englishmen might well feel proud; for there is, probably, no country in the world that possesses, in an equal degree, the raw material of national greatness. From all antiquity the land has been famed for its richness and fertility, yet for centuries it has been comparatively untouched and fallow. It possesses harbours on three seas, but they are entirely neglected. There are splendid rivers, but they have become useless for transport. Illimitable forests cover the mountains, but they are unproductive. Mines of coal, iron, copper, lead, and silver abound, but they are unworked. On

the Queen of the English collect a great fleet, let her stow away all her treasure, bullion, gold plate, and precious arms; be accompanied by all her court and chief people, and transfer the seat of her empire from London to Delhi. There she will find an immense empire ready made, a first-rate army, and a large revenue. I will take care of Syria and Asia Minor. The only way to manage the Afghans is by Persia and by the Arabs. We will acknowledge the Empress of India as our suzerain, and secure for her the Levantine coast. If she like, she shall have Alexandria, as she now has Malta: it could be arranged. And quite practicable; for the only difficult part, the conquest of India, which baffled Alexander, is all done!"

the announcement of the Anglo-Turkish Convention, it was stated that a new El-Dorado had been opened to the enterprise and energy of Englishmen; and it is quite true that, the conditions being favourable, there is scarcely any other country in the world which would offer so wide and profitable a field for British capital and industry as the possessions of the Sultan in Asia. But confidence is not a plant of rapid growth; the soil in which it takes root must be cultivated, and the atmosphere in which it grows must be genial. Capital cannot be productive in a country where justice, law, and order do not exist; and it is, therefore, idle to talk of directing enterprise into this new channel, until, at least, the elements from which confidence may ultimately spring shall have been first created.

It is very difficult to understand what the British Protectorate really means. Is it a Protectorate of the Turkish Pashas, or is it a Protectorate of the populations of Asiatic Turkey? If it is the former, then nothing but disaster will come of it; if the latter, then our Government must take the entire internal administration into its own hands. The Sultan's ministers will "accept" the reforms proposed by Sir Austin Layard, but those reforms will never be carried out. The position of Asiatic Turkey at the present moment is very similar to that of Egypt under the rule of the Mameluke Beys, who trampled on the rights of the people, and used all power for their own selfish ends. But Mehemet Ali, at one blow, struck down this tyranny, and from that day Egypt commenced to progress. The oligarchy that rules at Constantinople is not less corrupt and tyrannous, and as long as that rule lasts, there will be no hope of prosperity and peace for the down-trodden populations. I am very far from asserting that there are no honest men in the Grand Council of the Sultan, but they are in such a minority as to render their efforts useless; and even if, as his friends assert, the mantle of Fuad Pasha has fallen upon Midhat, he will not be able to succeed where Fuad and A'ali failed. Fuad was called a Ghiaour, and in the letter which he wrote to Abdul Aziz, from his death-bed at Nice, he said: "I know that the greater part of our Mussulmans will curse me as a Ghiaour and an enemy to our religion. I forgive their anger, for they can understand neither my sentiments nor my language. They will one day come to know that I, a Ghiaour, an 'impious innovator,' have been much more religious, much more truly a Mussulman, than the ignorant zealots who have covered me with their maledictions. They will recognize, but unhappily too late, that I have striven more than any other martyr to save the religion and the empire which they would have led to an inevitable ruin."* So it will be with Midhat if he attempt reforms in Asiatic Turkey. He will at once be branded with the name of Ghiaour, and may, possibly, meet with the same fate as has befallen Mehemet-Ali, in Albania. It should be remembered that the people in Asiatic Turkey have no part whatever in the government of the country. They are—Mussulmans, Jews, and Christians—mere slaves, subject to the caprice and passions of the ruling classes; and this army of vampires, who have lived on the life's blood of the "hewers of wood and drawers of water," will not give up their prescriptive rights to plunder and oppress without a determined struggle.

The utter hopelessness of the regeneration of Asiatic Turkey, by the Turks, is evident from the simple fact that the entire body politic is rotten from the head to the extremities. The whole art of government is all for self, and nothing for the country. Every one enrolled

* See Fuad Pasha's "Political Testament." Appendix II.

among the privileged brotherhood that prey upon the people, is permitted to do as he pleases, and men, without any regard to their qualifications, are promoted to the highest offices of the State. Mohammed Ruchdi Pasha, ex-Grand Vizier, was a private soldier, and he is now "*trois fois millionnaire.*" Riza Pasha, ex-Minister of War, was a grocer's boy in a shop at Stamboul, and every one in Constantinople knows the means by which he acquired the favour of Sultan Mahmoud. Mahmoud Pasha, ex-Grand Vizier, acquired an enormous fortune during his tenure of office as Minister of Marine; and Midhat Pasha himself was a poor man when he went as Governor-General to Bulgaria, but he returned one of the richest men in Europe. In most countries public functions are generally given to those who are deemed to be the most worthy. But it is otherwise in Turkey. The caprice of the Sovereign or his ministers, or the influence of the harem, can raise any one to the highest dignities without creating any astonishment or remark. If we were to go through the list of Grand Viziers, we would find in it men who had been *caïquedjies*, or boatmen; *bacals*, or grocers; *hamals*, or porters; charcoal burners, and carpet makers. "We might," says Prince Pitzipios, "take by chance a hundred individuals amongst the men invested with the highest positions in the State, and examine the means by which they have attained those dignities, and we would find that, with few exceptions, they were obtained through the caprice and the shameful passions of those who preside over the destinies of the nation."

It would be impossible to fully describe the corruption and peculation that prevails in Turkey. It exists in every department of the State, from the highest to the lowest. The *employés* are numbered by thousands, the majority of whom have been engaged in every menial occupation in the households of the different Pashas who have from time to time filled the post of Minister; these men are ill-paid, and are consequently obliged to secure a livelihood by any and every means at their command. No business can be transacted at a public department without bribing the subordinates, while the country is deprived of the muscle of a vast number of men who would be far more worthily occupied in tilling the soil, than in earning the right, by every conceivable baseness and humiliation, to watch for the crumbs that fall from the rich man's table. Every Pasha's house swarms with crowds of parasites, very few of whom receive regular wages, but the majority of whom are fed and clothed, getting every now and then an occasional backsheesh; all waiting until they can be placed in some public employment, to which they are no sooner nominated, than from unpaid servants they become wealthy functionaries of the State. Thus, menials of rich Pashas are preferred to provincial and district governments, or other civil posts; but before they have time to study, even if they were so inclined, the character, exigencies, and resources of the people and the country to which they are sent, or to learn the duties of their office, they are removed, or promoted to some new service, with an entire disregard to fitness, character, or education. A state of utter confusion prevails in every provincial administration, for no one knows the duties he is appointed to perform, while each new arrival has always a system peculiarly his own, diversified at times by some special instructions from his chiefs, or from Constantinople. The first aim of a governor of a province is to undo everything that has been done by his predecessor, and the second is to amass a fortune as speedily as possible. He knows that his tenure of office may be short, and, having neither patriotism nor honour, he goes in for plunder. He is at Aleppo to-day, to-morrow he may be at Beyrout. The prosperity of Aleppo is, therefore, of little consequence to him, and, accordingly, he sells justice to the highest bidder, so that he may be able to bribe the officials at the Porte. The disease which has eaten into the vitals of Turkey is widely spread, being rooted in the highest ranks of official life, and thence progressing in intensity to the lowest functionaries. It cannot be supposed that subordinate agents will be guided otherwise than by those around and immediately above them, and it is absurd to believe that, when the higher State functionaries are not imbued with more elevated notions of their respective duties and moral responsibilities, any hope of improvement among the lower can be expected.

A glance at the internal administration of Asiatic Turkey will show the difficulties of our Government in enforcing reforms, if these reforms are left to be carried out by the Turks.

Turkey in Asia is divided into vilayets, or governments-general, each of which is administered by a Pasha, who is nominated by the Porte. These vilayets are again divided into sandjaks, governed by kaïmakams, or lieutenant-governors. The sandjaks are subdivided into kasas, or districts, placed under the rule of mudirs, who frequently hold their appointment from the Governor-general, and the kasas, again, are divided into nahizéhs, composed of villages, or hamlets.

The mudirliks, many of which are without any fixed emoluments, and dependent upon precarious legal fees to render them remunerative are eagerly solicited, and are among the numerous sources of wealth which official position is heir to in Turkey. The nomination is usually left to the choice of provincial governors, subject to approval by the authorities at Constantinople, but it is supposed to be biassed by the wishes of the population of each division, when expressed by mansar or memorial. This, however, is frequently defeated, if ever attained, as the mudirlik, ostensibly the award of popular suffrage, is only too often the recompense of successful bribery or intrigue. For instance, a few of the most influential men of a kasa nominate one of their party for the mudirlik; a mansar or memorial is got up in his favour, to which the bulk of the population is forced to subscribe, and this memorial, backed by sundry douceurs, procures the appointment. In plain language, the place is sold; and the amount paid necessarily constitutes a tax, to be got back in some shape or form from the local population. Once confirmed in his post, the mudir cannot be arbitrarily removed by the Governor-general without sufficient cause being shown; but although it would be easy to procure evidence of the kind required, transgressions of the law, or neglect of duty, by public servants, are more frequently overlooked than punished, owing to the facility with which plenary indulgences for such offences may be purchased. The mudir's functions are purely executive, and he is responsible for the due transmission of the revenue when collected; though this branch of his duties is in most cases transferred to a saraff, or banker, who is usually one among those who have contributed to his nomination. Under these circumstances it may be readily imagined that the mudir is frequently a mere tool in the hands of a party, and his weakness and ignorance, constituting, perhaps, his strongest recommendation to office, contribute, when once invested with his new dignity, to make him the cypher contemplated by his supporters. Holding the executive power, he is responsible for all official acts of oppression within the kasa; but if, as is invariably the case, the medjlis, or local council, be with him, that body is ever ready to sanction his proceedings, and shield them by opportune masbatas and gilded arguments if by any chance they should be questioned by his superiors.

The mudir, by virtue of his office, presides at the medjlis, or local administrative council, which, besides the cadi, or legal authority, and the mufti, or priest, includes two or more azas, or deputies of the Christian faith, if the resident number duly qualify them for the privilege. These latter, however, dare not dissent from an opinion emitted by the Mussulman members. The medjlis meets twice a week for the discussion of local affairs, to receive complaints, and to judge all causes brought before it. Its *fiat* is not decisive, as the mudir may on his own responsibility refuse to execute its decisions. The council is, nevertheless, of great local importance; its members possess immense influence within their respective districts, and, under a corrupt and weak government, naturally all lean one way. Their whole study, with rare exceptions, is to decide, not on the justice or sanctity of the causes brought before them, or with reference to the general welfare of the community, but how they can best advance their own private interests, and escape clear of the intrigues that are constantly in movement around

H

them. Supported by his council, the mudir can act boldly; without the executive at command, the influence of the council would dwindle down to zero. Their interests being thus mutually blended, the medjlis of each kasa, with the addition of a few non-official men of weight, constitutes a camirilla, and holds in its hands the whole power—deliberative, judicial, financial, and executive—in the district.

The cadi is named by the Sheikh-ul-Islam, or chief of the Ulema, and can only be dismissed or removed by the same dignitary. At the Mékémé, or justice court, taking cognizance exclusively of suits judged by the Sherèat, or old law, he presides and decides summarily, giving his clam, or sentence, in writing. At the medjlis, which has jurisdiction on all cases indiscriminately, whether of the Sherèat or of the Canon, the cadi sits as local legal authority, subject to the correction of the mufti; and the Governor, or President of the Council, is bound to execute the sentence pronounced. The cadi usually joins the dominant party in the kasa, for to oppose it, when allied with the executive, would reduce him to a cypher, and sweep off most of his fees, or other precarious emoluments, as little or no attention would be paid to his decisions, which, when not evaded, under numerous pretences by the medjlis, would be unenforced by the executive. The natural consequence, then, would be, that few cases would be brought before his special tribunal, the Mékémé. On the other hand, to be at variance with the legal authority of the place would be highly inconvenient to the dominant party, by preventing many of their iniquitous deeds having a legal stamp upon them. Their mutual interests, therefore, attract them towards each other. Frequently, too, the ignorance and weakness of the mudir allows the cadi, with his superior endowments, to gain the ascendancy; and with the valuable cooperation of the medjlis, his power is then unbounded, and his means of acquiring wealth is restricted only by his conscience and the resources of the population. No registry is kept either of the discussions or decisions of the medjlis, although such records of its acts are required by law. Hence, two similar cases will frequently be decided differently, according to the interests to be decided by them. A decision at one sitting is not infrequently revoked or denied at another, and the most flagrant injustice is thus constantly committed with impunity, without the remotest chance of a reprimand or punishment. The decision of the medjlis may be referred to the higher provincial court, which, similarly constituted, affords little hope of redress. These appeals are, nevertheless, by no means of rare occurrence, and are encouraged by the provincial courts, as forming an important item of their emoluments. As the recognition of the legal claims of the weaker party would expose the other to severe censure or disgrace for dereliction of duty, so each party to a suit habitually prosecutes or defends his cause by the preliminary precaution of purchasing protection among the various members in power; and, naturally, the more wealthy of the litigants invariably carries the day, and crowns his triumph by the incarceration or reprimand of his antagonist.

In theory, the elective principle is at the base of the whole administrative system in Asiatic Turkey; but its influence for good is entirely set at naught by the corruption and venality existing at the seat of Government itself, which sanctions the grossest oppression and injustice. Enslaved by those whom the theory of the constitution has placed in the position of protectors, the peasantry have learned to submit; and those chosen from among them to fulfil the duties of guardians of the rights and liberties of their fellow-subjects, yield through fear to the orders of the governors. The judicial office, consequently, is everywhere prostituted, and the interests of the people are cruelly sacrificed.

The manner in which the taxes are collected affords another means of oppression; and when, as is usually the case, the tithe-farmer, backed by the mudir and saraff, combines with the cadi and medjlis, it may be easily conceived what powerful destructive engines may be brought to bear upon a hapless peasantry. In fact, it is the same dismal story throughout the country; the whole art and science of rural administration being to ring the changes upon the various State dues, and to tax ingenuity in devising new and patent modes of fleecing the people.

As punctuality in the transmission of all local contributions is the grand test of a governor's capabilities, so, provided the Imperial exchequer is not kept in arrears, it matters little what may be his other qualifications for the post. The mudir, therefore, has pretty much *carte blanche*, and the unfortunate peasant, taxed by the central Government, and cheated by its *employés*, is obliged to submit, or incur all the risk which springs from opposition. Should he, however, sue for redress, in the hope that from the administration of the law he will at least obtain the semblance of justice, what is the treatment in store for him? With the presentation of a memorial to the Vicegerent's Court, he gives utterance to his complaints. The memorial is received, and from the manner of its reception redress appears more than probable. The requisite information is obtained, and the whole bearing of the question apparently sifted. His accusation made, the peasant must enter into bonds for the consequences. The mudir, or offending party, is then sent for, but the bombashee cannot somehow prevail on any of the plaintiff's witnesses to come forward; cautioned and forewarned, they deny all knowledge of the case. The mudir and his subordinates already chuckle at the certain discomfiture of the foe, and the poor peasant is dismayed at the altered tone in which he is addressed. The defendant, supported by numerous suborned witnesses, brings counter-charges against the plaintiff, and these charges are sure to be confirmed by the never-failing mazbata.* Some member of the medjlis,

* The mazbata is a petition against an individual. It is seldom the voluntary result of independent action, but more frequently is obtained by threats, or through fear of the authorities.

perhaps, feebly espouses his cause, to be overruled by his colleagues; this is quite orthodox and regular. The case is dead against the plaintiff, who is imprisoned for penalties inconsiderately incurred, and punished for slandering his superiors. Such is the ordinary course of justice, diversified at times by the complainant's intention of appeal becoming known, when it is summarily swamped by a course of prison and courbash that speedily brings him to his senses.

In many sections of the country the resident proprietary have been entirely stripped of all moveable capital, and have nothing remaining but the bare land, and the miserable roof that affords but nominal protection against the inclemencies of the weather; and these are heavily encumbered with debt. Reduced to this pitiable state, the prosecution of their farming labours becomes impracticable, and they are consequently compelled to obtain relief by a system which virtually converts them into the bondsmen of the usurers enriched by their prostration. The usurer—banker or merchant, according to the title he may assume—enters into a stipulation with the elders of a village, whereby, for certain considerations, he engages to supply the villagers with funds and materials necessary for agricultural purposes. In thus constituting himself the village banker, he charges a monthly interest on his running account, and takes his reimbursement out of the produce raised,—with the option, if the value of such produce exceeds the debt, of appropriating the whole at opening prices. Accordingly, he furnishes seed, provender, and all the materials for domestic and agricultural use, loaded with a premium of fifty to a hundred per cent., and advances the money which may from time to time be requisite for payment of taxes and other incidental claims,— exacting interest for each advance at rates varying from two to five and six per cent. per month. To such a dependent state are the farmers reduced that they are frequently without oxen or ploughs, and these are sold to them, in the ploughing season, by the banker, for a stated sum, bearing a monthly interest, and afterwards repurchased at a fifth or sixth part of the amount. When the crops are matured and the villagers assemble to fix the opening prices, if the usurer remains without a competitor—as is usually the case,— the produce passes into his hands at so low a valuation that it is impossible to discharge his claims; and thus a portion of his advances remains in the form of a permanent debt, which enables him to impose more onerous conditions for the ensuing season. If competitors should offer for the produce, and threaten to drive up the opening prices—a circumstance that rarely happens—he demands immediate restitution of his advances, with the alternative of arrest and imprisonment; and, what may appear incredible, he actually possesses the power to imprison at once every male in the village. Unless, therefore, his rivals are themselves prepared to acquit the debt, their superior offers are rejected, and they are compelled to retire from the field. This is the more easy to enforce, as the varied crops in Asiatic Turkey being matured at different periods of the year, the value of ready produce for which the casual buyer bids will not cover the aggregate disbursements or cancel the claims of the local banker. Thus the village debt is never liquidated, and varies in amount according as good or bad harvests predominate; the inevitable result being that the whole of the fixed productive property eventually changes hands. In some sandjaks, whole districts, and in others detached villages are in this deplorable condition, and once entangled in the meshes of these usurers, the independence of the peasantry is irrevocably lost.

Such is the unhappy condition of the people of Asiatic Turkey,—Mussulmans as well as Christians—the whole administration, in fact, being so arranged that the entire agricultural population is a prey to the usurer, the tax-farmer, and the Turkish officials. Thus it will be seen how difficult is the task undertaken by our Government. No reforms are possible, if their execution be left exclusively in the hands of the Turks; and without the direct supervision of British administrators, all attempts at reform will prove futile. To create order out of this chaos, to establish the reign of justice where hitherto it has not existed, to give liberty—civil and religious—to a down-trodden people, is a noble ambition; but it will be a Herculean labour. The British statesman, however, who succeeds in its accomplishment, will earn the gratitude of millions of human beings, and make for himself a name in history that will last as long as the Pyramids.

CHAPTER XI.

RESOURCES OF ASIATIC TURKEY.

THE actual statistics relative to the mineral resources of Asiatic Turkey are very limited, although its mineral wealth is known to be great and varied. The mines of Asia Minor are famed in history for their richness, and, although their prosperity declined with the civilization to the necessities of which they ministered, the strata where the ores lie imbedded still remain, and only await the advent of steam, skill, and capital to furnish tangible proof of their undoubted value. At the present time, silver and lead are extensively found in the Asiatic division of the Empire, and the Taurus range is celebrated for the abundance of its copper. Coal is also found in the districts of Asia Minor forming the southern coast of the Black Sea. It is, however, quite impossible to estimate the extent of the coal measures in

Asia Minor, as the only coal-field of which we have any definite information is that in the neighbourhood of Heraclia. In this district, the mineral crops out on the surface, and the seams, which vary in thickness from three to eighteen feet, have been inexpensively worked by adits into the side of the mountain; but, through unskilful working, they do not give, either in quantity or quality, a tenth part of what they are capable. The best coal has hitherto been procured from the valley of Kosloo, which is in immediate vicinity to the coast, and most eligibly suited for coaling vessels from shoots, without any intermediate boat carriage. The Kosloo could, without any extraordinary effort, yield about thirty thousand tons of coal per annum, and of a quality equal to the very best Newcastle, having a loss of only seven per cent. in clinker and ashes.

In the valley of Soungoul, which adjoins Kosloo, the coal seams are from nine to twelve feet in thickness, and the coal itself is quite equal in quality to, and much harder than, the Kosloo. In fact, the whole of the Soungoul valley contains excellent coal, which might be shipped in the same way as Kosloo, without the necessity of boating off. This important coal district is situated about 130 miles from the entrance to the Bosphorus, and is in every respect most eligibly situated for water transport; but the unhealthiness of the place, arising from malaria generated by undrained lands, is a serious drawback to continuous operations. The coal at Kosloo is brought to grass at about six shillings per ton, but, being rather soft in grain, is much deteriorated in quality when it reaches market, owing to the clumsy and unworkmanlike manner in which it is manipulated by the natives, who alone are available for the work. In forming an opinion, however, as to the value of Heraclia coal, it is necessary to remember the surface character of the mineral, and the mixture of inferior with superior sorts inseparable from an extensive employment of unskilled labour. The coal is easy to win, and is large and merchantable. In depth, the quality will without doubt improve, while if steam colliers were employed in its transport, instead of the small sailing craft now in use, a marked difference would soon be observable in the size and general appearance of the coal when delivered for consumption. This splendid property will, however, remain unproductive to the Government until foreign enterprise is invited to do that, for the accomplishment of which the capital and industry of the country itself is inadequate.

The metalliferous minerals are also comparatively unworked. No less than eighty-two mines of various ores have been discovered, but of this number few are now in operation; and of these, not one is worked to the full limits of its capacity. Five silver mines, one of lead, and four of copper, were six years ago worked by the Government— the first only producing about 570,000 okes, the second 175,000, and the third 965,000. Of the mines worked by private persons, those of Eléon, near Trebizond, yield 250,000 okes of copper, and those of Tokat, 300,000. In the year 1862, more than 440,000 kilos. of copper, valued at about 1,000,000 francs, were shipped to France. The copper mines of Bakyrkurchai, which in the time of Mahmoud II., enabled Ismail Bey, the then Turcoman chief of Sinope, to pay a yearly tribute of 200,000 ducats, are now completely neglected. The mines of Tireboli, which formerly, under very bad management, yielded from 150 to 200 tons of copper annually, are now practically unproductive, though possessing every advantage of situation and abundant fuel that mining enterprise could require. The silver mines of Gumush-

Khaneh, near Trebizond, once the most famous of all the silver mines in Asia, are now also nearly forsaken, their annual net produce seldom averaging more than 90 lbs. The only mine in Asia anything like a success is the well-known Argana-Madén, which produces nearly 400 tons of copper annually. The average ores in this mine contain 12 to 15 per cent. of pure metal, and the profits, under good management, ought to be considerable. The mines of Bulgar-Dagh, on the slopes of the Taurus, are also exceedingly rich; the ores containing 21 per cent. of lead, giving 428 grammes of silver and four of gold per 100 kilogrammes. The yield at present is trifling, but the mines are capable, under improved management and with good machinery, of producing 12,000 tons annually, while the cost of extraction is estimated at only 30 francs 50 cents. per ton. Argentiferous galena exists also in great plenty at Akdagh-Madén, in the district of Tokat; but though the veins crop up in the very midst of forests, and labour is cheap and abundant, little of the ore is at present utilized.

On the slope of the Ishik-Dagh, in the pashalic of Angora, similar wealth invites enterprise; as also again at Desek-Madén, in the same province, within ten miles of the river Kissil-Irmak. At Eléhen, too, some twenty miles south of Tireboli, large deposits of copper ore are known to exist, but no effort has been made to turn the discovery to account; while at the silver mines of Esseli, Kuré-Madén, and Helveli, the method of working is so defective that the resultant yield for the whole is only a yearly total of some 250 tons.

The agricultural resources of Syria and Asia Minor are also very great, but those which remain dormant are so vast as to be practically unlimited. The whole stretch of country between the Syrian coast-range and the Euphrates is capable of cotton production to an extent hardly conceivable, except by those who are acquainted with the topography of the district, while the uncultivated area of Asia Minor is also very large. The natural advantages possessed by these provinces, in their climate and geographical position, are enjoyed by few other countries in the world, and enormous tracts, where water is plentiful and the soil most fruitful, might be easily obtained; and when it is considered that Turkey in Asia has an area of six hundred and seventy-three thousand seven hundred and forty-six square miles, with a population of but sixteen millions and fifty thousand, giving only 23·8 to the square mile, it may be imagined what a vast extent of fertile land is there lying unproductive. For example, the Pashalic of Damascus, which extends, North to South, from Hamah on the Orontes down to the deserts of Arabia Petræa, south-east of the Dead Sea—a length of about four degrees of latitude—is capable of supporting a population of six millions of souls, whereas, at present, the population is not more than five hundred thousand. There is, however, little room for labourers or artizans; it is the wide spread of uncultivated land, and that only, which affords a field to foreign settlers, and it is, therefore, to agriculture that immigrants should direct their energies.*

Next to the possession of some practical knowledge of agriculture, and intelligence to apply it to local circumstances, capital, sufficient for the work he proposes to undertake, is the first requisite for an immigrant. His land will cost him little, but he will find no buildings on it, and working stock and implements have to be purchased. He will require, moreover, about three times as much arable land as, with the same views regarding extent of culture, he

* See Appendix III.

would undertake in England. Because, 1st, manure cannot be purchased; 2nd, the raising or fattening of stock does not assume the prominence in Turkish which it does in English farming; 3rd, the manure made by his working stock will be in full demand for the portion of the farm amenable to irrigation; therefore, bare fallow has, as a rule, to supply the place of manure, and due allowance for this must be made in the area of land obtained or purchased. Further, no immigrant farmer should trust altogether to native labourers; not only would their comparative apathy thwart the energy he might himself possess, but their "feast-days" would be a perpetual hindrance to him whether they were Moslems or Christians. He should, therefore, take with him a sufficient staff of labourers, with their families, to conduct the ordinary work of the farm; if possible, making the enterprise a co-operative one. Then, he should also bear in mind that grain-growing, though comparatively a tame pursuit, to an enterprising man, is almost a certainty in Syria and Asia Minor, and that, with ordinary care, it is fairly remunerative; but that cotton, tobacco, sesame, flax, and other summer crops, though perhaps more tempting, require special study and local experience. The culture of the vine and wine-making, as well as that of the mulberry and rearing of silkworms—if undertaken with an adequate amount of knowledge—are, however, quite as safe as grain-farming, and much more profitable. It would be useless for an isolated person to attempt to make his way; but by co-operation in large bodies, composed of British capitalists and workmen, success might be looked upon as certain.

Major G. de Winton, in his account of "A Visit to a Model Farm in Asia Minor," published in *Fraser's Magazine*, gives the following details of the profits on grain-farming:—"The farm of Arab-Tchiftlik," he says, "was purchased by the father of the present proprietor, fifteen years ago, for one thousand pounds sterling. It contains about ten thousand acres, of which upwards of four thousand are now under cultivation. There are two villages on the estate— one on the south, and the other on the north side of a promontory; the population of the two together being about fifteen hundred. The distance from Smyrna by water is about six hours, and by land, five hours by mule. The inhabitants are all Greeks; the Kavasses or guards, ten in number, only being Turks. The number of acres in cultivation is—wheat, 1500; barley, 500; vines, 100; garden crops, 2100. Of live stock, there are 4000 sheep; 400 horned-cattle, and 200 horses. The mode of letting the land is as follows:—The land is let in small farms of 30, 60, and 90 acres for wheat or barley; and half the corresponding number of acres for garden produce. The seed is given by the landlord, who receives one-half the produce in kind; one-tenth in kind is paid to the Government as tithe. The average price of wheat is 3s. 6d. a bushel. The account of a man farming thirty acres would stand as under:—

30 acres, at 18 bushels an acre: 540 bush. at 3s. 6d. £99 10 0	To landlord (one-half) £72 5 0
15 acres of spring and garden crops (average). . . . 45 0 0	To Government . . 7 4 6
	Balance . . . 65 0 6
£144 10 0	£144 10 0

In general a man farms about ninety acres; keeping two farm servants, to whom he pays wages £8 and including rations, about £20 a year. In this case the account would stand thus:—

90 acres, at 18 bushels an acre: 1620 bush. at 3s. 6d. £298 10 0	To landlord . . £216 15 0	
45 acres of spring crops, at £3 an acre 135 0 0	To Government . 20 5 0	
	Two Servants at £20 each . . . 40 0 0	
	Balance . . . 156 10 0	
£433 10 0	£433 10 0	

Sheep are taken upon the following terms:— The owner gives the sheep and grazing ground, receiving twenty-five per cent. in cash as the value of the sheep yearly; the farmer being bound to return an equal number of sheep at the expiration of the contract. Mr. B—— has expended a large sum on his property. In the southern village he has built a handsome Greek church, capable of containing four hundred persons, at a cost of £2500, and he has also established schools in both villages. So far as I was able to judge from the short period I remained at Arab-Tchiftlik, the villagers appeared to be in a more prosperous condition than that of any of the labouring classes I have seen in this or in any other country, with the exception, perhaps, of New South Wales. The requirements of the people are few, and drunkenness is a crime but little known. The population is rapidly increasing, the land under cultivation increases every year, and one hundred acres have just been apportioned for making vineyards. The village has a priest and a doctor, but no lawyer. The intendant arranges small disputes; graver cases are referred to Mr. B——, who settles them on the occasion of his periodical visits; and if I may judge from his decisions in general by those given on the occasion of my visit, I should say they were satisfactory to all, as both parties appeared to go away contented. The rentals of the estate are now between £2000 and £3000 a year. . . . I should mention that the farm of Arab-Tchiftlik is perhaps the only one of its kind in Asia Minor, and I fear there are but few proprietors like Mr. B——. The experiment made by him is, however, a very interesting one, and proves that, with a little attention, farming can be carried on in Asiatic Turkey with great advantage both to the landlord and tenant. There are thousands of acres of rich lands, now untilled, to be bought at a nominal price, which the Turk will not, and the rayah cannot, cultivate." *

There is, besides, scarcely any country in the

---

* I have recently received offers for the sale of fertile land in Palestine and Syria, most eligibly situated for colonization.

world which offers so wide and profitable a field for British capital and industry as the possessions of the Turks in Asia. Good roads and inexpensive railways are required to improve the communications between existing business centres, and open up vast tracts of country which have, at present, no outlet for their products. The obstacles to the navigation of many rivers demand removal, so as to facilitate the transit of produce from the interior. Wharves require to be built to save costly transhipment of merchandise; tracts of country to be drained in order to bring them into proper condition for the growth of cotton; towns to be lighted and cleansed; agriculture and manufactures encouraged, and the immense mineral wealth of the country developed. Here then is a vast field for British skill and capital; and which we may now command. The future of Palestine, Syria, and Asia Minor is in our hands, and it depends upon our Government whether these splended countries shall still remain a comparative desert, or whether they shall be thrown open to foreign enterprise that will not only enrich those whose labour and capital are expended, but also contribute to the happiness and prosperity of the populations themselves. One thing is wanting,—that the rule of the Turkish Pashas should cease, and a reign of law, justice, and liberty should take its place. Then would revive the ancient grandeur of the Khalifs. The Tigris and Euphrates would again water cities equal to the Nineveh and Babylon that once stood upon their banks. A new Tadmor would rival the glories of Palmyra. The Orontes would carry treasures to a restored Antioch, the "Star of the East." Smyrna would once more become the "Gem of Asia;" and the maritime cities of Syria would recall the splendours of Sidon and of Tyre.

CHAPTER XII.

RAILWAYS IN ASIATIC TURKEY.

It is hardly possible to point to an instance in which the injury caused by defective appliances for the transport of merchandise exceeds that from which Asiatic Turkey is at present suffering. In its effects, the state of the transit has the same tendency as the inland and export duties, in narrowing the circle of the country's productive capabilities. Hence wheat and other commodities which might, under more favourable circumstances, be brought down to the ports, have, in some places, a mere local value. Instances are numerous where the population have been in a state of comparative famine in one part of the country from scarcity of breadstuffs, while in others, wheat, &c., might be purchased at nearly nominal prices. In two particular cases, it has been estimated that to bring grain down 36 and 150 miles, the average cost of transport was respectively 4s. and 16s. per quarter, whereas over good roads this sum might be reduced to 1s. and 4s. a quarter; the difference being upwards of 13 and 112 per cent. on the farmer's gross receipts.

In dealing, however, with the means of transport and communication in Turkey, a grave error has been committed by railway *concessionnaires*, who have misled the public by apparently splendid schemes, and induced capitalists to embark their money in enterprises which carried with them the seeds of their own failure. It is fatal to such undertakings to judge them by the standard of results in England, and other equally advanced countries. The scale of such works is far too much in advance of the state of agricultural development; whereas a good system of narrow-gauge railways would at once induce an immense increase of traffic, and would not require the costly outlay necessary in the ordinary railway system. Such railways have already been adopted in Russia, Sweden, Norway, Australia, New Zealand, India, and South America; while in the United States of America, narrow-gauge railways have been commenced, or are being projected, in almost every State and territory from the eastern to the western seaboard. The Ottoman Railway (Smyrna to Aidin), 80 miles, was built at a cost of £1,784,000 or £22,300 per mile; the Smyrna and Cassaba, 61 miles, £800,000, or £13,115 a mile; the Varna and Rustchuk, 140 miles, £2,158,975, or £15,421 a mile; while in America, the Denver and Rio Grande narrow-gauge railway, running from Denver, in Colorado, to the city of Mexico—1750 miles in length—has not, except in the mountain districts, exceeded 14,000 dollars a mile, including stations, engine and carriage buildings, workshops, &c. If this latter system were adopted in Asiatic Turkey, there would be little difficulty in obtaining the capital required to build her railways. In fact, the introduction of such a system must precede any further great increase of trade; and as the safety of investments depends upon the power of the debtor to pay, it is obvious that any means which can tend to augment that power on the part of the Porte must operate as an additional guarantee for the faithful observance of its obligations.

In that portion of Asia Minor from which the great bulk of the exported produce is drawn— and of which Samsoun on the Black Sea and Smyrna on the Mediterranean are the principal shipping ports—the roads are everywhere in a most primitive condition, and, during the winter months, in many parts almost unavailable. The whole of the Samsoun district, which may be described by straight lines drawn from Samsoun to Sivas, thence to Angora, and northward again to Sinope, is celebrated for its fetility; yet there is not a single trunk road in the entire area. Immense quantities of grain, as well as tobacco and other produce, could be raised in the interior; but, without the means of transport, profitable cultivation is out of the question. The port of Samsoun is capable of being made one of the best in the Black Sea, and its exports should not be less in importance than those of Odessa; but in order to effect any great improvement in the harbour, so as to render it safe and commodious, engineering works of rather an extensive character would be necessary.

Northern Anatolia has a practical monopoly of the transit trade with Persia, but although this trade yields an important revenue, and the country itself, if even partially cultivated, would largely increase the income from the tithe, there was not until very recently a good road over which produce could be safely transported through the winter months. There is a road which enters

Kars from Russia, passes through to Erzeroum, and, dividing thence, branches north to Trebizond, and, in a westerly direction, to Tokat; but, with the exception of the Trebizond road, these are mere bridle tracks, carried sometimes through swamps, and sometimes over mountain summits. The valleys of the Tcharaki and Raibut are all that could be desired, and, at intervals not far removed, there are depressions in the mountain chains through which roads could be carried without involving the necessity of works of an expensive character. But road-making is not the *forte* of the Turks. The Trebizond road took twenty years to make, and its history is remarkable. It was commenced in 1852 by Ismail Pasha, but, with the exception of two or three kilomètres outside Trebizond, the project remained in abeyance until 1864. The small piece made in 1852, together with the repair of the old road as far as Khosh-oglan, a town two hours from Trebizond, cost the Government no less than ten millions of piastres, a sum that frightened them out of completing the work. In 1864, however, they took heart of grace, and a body of European engineers was despatched to survey the route and recommence the works. From 1864 to 1868, a length of twenty kilomètres was finished, and about 350 more surveyed. The estimate for the completion of the road was fixed at seventy millions of piastres, but the Porte thought the estimate too high, and the engineers were recalled. About this time, however, Mustapha Pasha, Mushir of the 4th Army Corps (Anatolia), being at Constantinople, undertook the construction of the road, on the *corvée* system, within four years, for the sum of ten millions of piastres. The conditions were accepted, and the Pasha started for Trebizond, and, within the given time, completed the road. Owing to the completion of this road, the Persian transit trade must necessarily for some time to come remain in possession of Turkey. But as soon as the projected railway shall be constructed from Batoum to Kars, and thence by Erivan to Tabreez, the merchants of Erzeroum and Trebizond will find that their trade and profits have departed.

With numerous roadsteads on the south side of the Black Sea, Turkey does not possess one really good harbour; and although roads from the interior to the coast would be in themselves an inestimable blessing to the population, yet they would be to a large extent useless without proper harbours for the shipment of surplus produce. If it were possible to complete a good road from Samsoun to Sivas; to clear out the river Sakaria—which waters a country between Angora and the Black Sea, abounding in natural riches of the most varied character— and to canalize fifty miles of the Sarabat, which flows into the Gulf of Smyrna, the resulting advantages both to the people and the Government would be so apparent that an impetus would be given to the initiation of similar works elsewhere, and less difficulty be experienced in their accomplishment. The Maritza, the Orontes, the Jordan, and other rivers in Asia Minor and Syria might, in little more than a twelvemonth, be cleared from the snags and sandbanks which now render them useless for transport, and float down such wealth of produce to the sea as would enrich the population and all concerned in this development of the country's splendid resources.

A great portion of the produce of Anatolia intended for export is brought to Smyrna for shipment; yet from this latter point, again, the roads into the interior are at times impassable. At the best they are suited for camel transit alone; and, but for the construction of the two lines of railway—the Aidin and the

Cassaba—the prospects of the Smyrna trade would be anything but satisfactory. Whatever may be the result, however, in respect of the profits which may be earned by these lines, the policy of encouraging the formation of expensive railways, while the roads in the interior remain in their present condition is, to say the least, questionable. If the same amount of energy and capital had been expended on road construction as have been spent on the Aidin and the Cassaba railways, the trade of Smyrna would ere this have been sensibly increased by an influx of produce from districts which are at present practically shut out from the seaboard.

Beyrout, which is the port of Mount Lebanon and Damascus—in fact, the principal maritime outlet for Syria—is in a deplorable condition, as far as harbour accommodation is concerned. The port is simply an open roadstead, from which ships have frequently to run for shelter; all goods require to be lightered from vessels riding at anchor, and there is not accommodation at the custom-house for the goods which are at times discharged. The damage done to property by reason of insufficient landing facilities is frequently a severe tax on importers, while the risk, consequent on the lighterage of cargo, is such as should not be imposed on any mercantile community. Yet there would be no difficulty in the construction of an efficient breakwater and a commodious quay, to the cost of which the merchants of Beyrout are quite willing to contribute. Jaffa, too, which is the southernmost port in Syria, and the *entrepôt*, for Jerusalem, Nablous, Gaza, and the interior of Palestine, is without any satisfactory harbour accommodation. The only landing-place, both for passengers and goods, is a very unsuitable erection of a few feet in length. There is a natural breakwater eight hundred feet long, but it is so silted up as to be available only for coasting craft, larger vessels being obliged to anchor in the roadstead. That the port of Jaffa is capable of being made good and safe for vessels of average sea-going tonnage does not admit of doubt, and works of substantial and enduring character could easily be undertaken. A railway, or well-made road, between Jaffa and Jerusalem would be a great boon to the travelling public, as well as to the thousands of pilgrims who annually toil over the track by which the two places are connected. A good road is also much wanted from Nablous on the north, and from Kerek across the ford of the

K

Dead Sea, through Gaza, on the south; such roads as these running into Jaffa would be of material service in the transport of produce. If the port were put in good condition, with a new breakwater and serviceable quays, and a road driven in a north-easterly direction by way of Nablous into the Pashalic of Damascus, Jaffa would soon become a great emporium of trade.

Well-made roads, good canals, and inexpensive railways are *desiderata* for Asiatic Turkey, as so long as the present defective system of internal communication exists, the full development of the country's agricultural resources must be seriously retarded. Rivers, harbours, and highways there may be in abundance; but if the first of these be simply tortuous torrents, the second a compound of mud and gullies, and the third mere bridle paths, composed of iron-bound ruts in summer, and all but impassable sloughs of mud in winter, their utility is but of minimum value. Good roads, serviceable canals, and economically-made railways are, besides, civilizing agents of the highest order, while, on the other hand, their absence restrains enterprise, diverts trade, and lessens cultivation. When locomotion is slow, expensive, and at times impossible, community of interest and sentiment in the population is effectually prevented; the different parts of the machinery of government cannot work in unison, and the entire community languishes for want of arterial circulation. Of what value are bursting fields of cotton if the cost of transport would render its shipment to a foreign market profitless? None; for in such a case poverty must be the fate of the cultivator. It is in vain to issue edicts having for their object the amelioration of the common lot, if the producer is unable to place his commodities within reach of the consumer; and it is equally futile to expect any great increase in the revenue of the State when merely the coast line of the Empire is capable of effective utilization. A string of laden camels wending its way from the interior of Anatolia to the coast is not an edifying spectacle in these modern days; nor is one of the loaded skin-rafts of the Tigris, floating on the current from Diarbekhr to Bagdad, in any sense a proper substitute for the means of carriage which engineering science could provide. It is true that efforts have from time to time been made by the Porte in the construction of roads; but, either from the fact that imperial interests have been made subservient to individual aggrandisement, or that the difficulties of the task have been under-estimated, these efforts have almost invariably resulted in disappointment. Effective administration of the internal affairs of an empire, and defective means of communication between its several parts, cannot co-exist. Practically, justice cannot be administered in a community where an appeal to the source from which it flows is a physical impossibility; while without transit facilities for barter, the intelligent skill of a people is worthless, and the accumulation of individual wealth impracticable. So evenly balanced, however, are the topographical advantages of Turkey in Asia, that there is no one spot so situated as to preclude the transport of its produce to a profitable market, provided there exist good roads and railways, serviceable canals, and renovated sea-ports.

CHAPTER XIII.

THE EUPHRATES VALLEY RAILWAY.

THE British Protectorate of Asiatic Turkey has again directed attention to the great enterprise of an iron highway from the Mediterranean or the Bosphorus to the Persian Gulf, which has been for more than five-and-twenty years before the public. Three projects have been proposed with this view; the first, that of the Euphrates Valley route, proposed by General Chesney, Sir John Macneill, and Mr. W. P. Andrew; the second (though latest in order of time), that of Mr. Latham; and the third, the grander if more difficult scheme of Sir Macdonald Stephenson. The first, so long and ably agitated by Mr. Andrew, has never, I believe, been put forward as one likely in itself to be remunerative, but rather as an undertaking essential to our own national interests. Mr. Latham's modification of the scheme, although undoubtedly possessing some special merits, has hitherto lacked the influential sponsorship necessary to its success; while Sir Macdonald Stephenson's great enterprise was deemed by many an impossibility, as, at the time it was mooted, no more advanced European starting-point could be found than Vienna. Now, however, that the Roumelian railway will in time unite the Straits of Dover with the Bosphorus, half the practical argument against Sir Macdonald's project will be removed, and it is fast becoming probable that the prophecy made by him, twenty years ago, will be an accomplished fact before the world is another decade older.

The practicability of the Euphrates Valley route was early demonstrated by a costly survey made by Sir John Macneill and General Chesney; but doubts as to its commercial prospects discouraged Her Majesty's Government from giving the guarantee, without which capitalists refused the means to carry it out. The scheme, as first projected by General Chesney and Sir John Macneill, involved departure from Europe at Trieste or Brindisi, whence steamers would run to Suedia on the coast of Syria. Thence, a line of railway would be carried up the Orontes valley to Antioch, and on by Aleppo to Ja'ber Castle on the Euphrates, and finally down to the confluence of the latter river with the Tigris at Kurnah. From this point, a line of powerful steamers would continue the communication to Kurrachee on the Indus, from which place railways are now complete to Bombay, Madras, Calcutta, and the North-Western provinces of India. Pending the development of the expected river traffic, however, it was proposed to lay down the railway over only the first section of the route, from the Mediterranean to Ja'ber Castle, whence a fleet of steamers would continue the communication to Kurnah and Bussorah. By this line, the estimated saving of time between London and Calcutta would be about sixteen or seventeen days—once the railway was complete.*

* In the report of the Select Committee appointed to examine the subject of railway communication between the Mediterranean and the Persian Gulf, published in 1872, it was stated that "the sum of £10,000,000 would be amply sufficient to cover the expenses of the shortest route." At that time, I received an offer from a combination of contractors and capitalists, who were prepared to make the railroad, on the narrow-gauge system, and to carry it from Alexandretta, on the Mediterranean, viâ Aleppo, to Bussorah, at the head of the Persian Gulf, for the sum of £5,000,000, or half the amount of the lowest estimate mentioned by the committee, and to guarantee an average

The route proposed by Mr. Latham was to be from Alexandretta, instead of Suedia, and thence, by the Beilan Pass and Antioch, to Aleppo, and across the Euphrates at Birejik. But whereas the original scheme of Messrs. Andrew, Chesney, and Macneill turned sharp down the river valley from Ja'ber Castle, through the arid wastes of the south, Mr. Latham proposed to go, at the cost of some two hundred miles of increased distance, through Northern Mesopotamia, past Orfa, Mardin, Jezireh, Mosul, and Bagdad; hitting the Gulf at Kurnah or Bussorah—in fact, the established post and caravan route through a settled and cultivated country. This line would, as I have stated, be some two hundred miles longer than that projected by General Chesney, but it would, on the other hand, have commercial advantages over the latter, which would amply counterbalance the trifling difference of time and extra cost of construction involved.

Alexandretta, besides, is a fine natural harbour, easily made at all times, and affording

speed of thirty-five miles an hour. I submitted this offer to the Turkish Government, by whom it was referred to the Turkish Ambassador in London; but his Excellency expressed to me his dissatisfaction at this offer having been made to the Porte.

shelter in nearly every state of the wind, while it is, at the same time, the long-established outlet for Northern Syria, through which the vast transit traffic of the interior has passed for ages. A small outlay on drainage would render it as healthy as any point along the coast; while, inland, Beilan presents no considerable engineering difficulties whatever. Eastwards, too, Mr. Latham's proposed line would have many and weighty advantages over that by the Euphrates. The latter, whether it were opened up first by river navigation—the practicability of which is, to say the least, doubtful—or, at once, by a line of railway throughout, would run through a comparatively desert country, devoid of trade, and at the mercy of the predatory Arabs. In fact, for many years, it would have to depend mainly, if not entirely, on its through Indian traffic for support.

Mr. Latham's route, on the contrary, would run through a populous and commercially active chain of provinces, past thriving towns, and with resources for increasing trade everywhere abundant. Mosul and Bagdad—not to mention Diarbekhr, which would be rendered tributary by a good branch tramway—are *emporia* in themselves sufficient to feed a cheaply constructed and carefully managed line. The actual distance, it is true, by this route would be some two hundred miles greater; but this would be more than compensated for by its immense relative advantages of abundant and cheap labour, and of material for making the line throughout; as well as by the trade and industrial activity already in vigorous existence along its whole extent, from Scanderoon to the Gulf—in addition to the Indian traffic, which would certainly not be less than by the torrid solitudes of the Euphrates.

The grand idea, however, of Sir Macdonald Stephenson, which, twenty years ago, was deemed little more than a splendid chimera, sinks now to the level of practicable commonplace in these days of Indo-European and Trans-Atlantic telegraphy. In fact, by the progress already made in its fulfilment since it was first enunciated by its eminent promoter, the project may be said to be almost half achieved. The original scheme of Sir Macdonald contemplated a continuous chain of railways from Calais to Calcutta, traversing Europe to the Bosphorus, and hence across Asia Minor to Persia, Beloochistan, and the Indus; and, now that the Roumelian railway is progressing—which was the first part of Sir Macdonald's idea—the second section, or, at least, that portion of it from the Bosphorus to the Persian Gulf, should re-attract attention. In an able pamphlet on railway communication with India, published by Professor Chenery, the line is shown to be not only practicable, but inexpensive. Some parts of the route have already been surveyed. A short piece from Scutari to Ismidt has been thoroughly done, and more than one route has been examined into the interior in the direction of Eski-Shehr, Angora, and Afiun Kara-Hissar. The line now suggested is by Ismidt, Kutahia, Afiun Kara-Hissar, Konieh, Ak-Seraï, Yeni-Shehr, Kaisaria, and Aleppo. The most difficult part of the line would be that between Ismidt and Kutahia or Eski-Shehr, where there would be a section, happily of not more than ten miles, on which the works would necessarily be of an expensive character.

From Afiun Kara-Hissar, however, to the northern base of the Taurus there is no extraordinary difficulty. That portion lying to the north-east of Alexandretta has not yet been surveyed, but although this is, perhaps, the most difficult part of the line, there is nothing in it which may not be easily accomplished, at no excessive cost, in the present state of science. From Aleppo to the Persian Gulf the route is almost a complet flat, and the only addition to the cost of the works would arise from the necessity of crossing the various affluents of the Euphrates, which, although nearly dried up in the summer, roll a considerable torrent in the rainy season of the year. The entire line, constructed with proper solidity, and capable of bearing traffic at a high rate of speed, might, it is estimated, be made through the whole of Asiatic Turkey, from the Bosphorus to the Persian Gulf, for £12,000 to £15,000 a mile.

The distance between London and Constantinople, on the completion of the Roumelian Railway, will be traversed in one hundred hours. On the Asiatic portion of the line, assuming it to be well constructed, the trains might easily travel at an average of twenty-five miles an hour, including stoppages, and that, for the distance, one thousand five hundred miles, between the Bosphorus and Bussorah, would give sixty hours,—a total of one hundred and sixty hours, or six days sixteen hours from London to the Gulf. It is suggested that the railway should be continued, in course of time, to Bunder Abbas, otherwise Gombroon, a place now belonging to the Imaum of Muscat, and formerly the seat of a considerable trade.

The distance from Bussorah to Bunder Abbas is seven hundred miles, which, at twenty-five miles an hour, would be traversed in twenty-eight hours. Add to this, the hundred and sixty hours before mentioned, and we have the duration of the whole transit between London and Bunder Abbas—one hundred and eighty-eight hours, or seven days twenty hours. From Bunder Abbas to Kurrachee, along the coast, is a distance of seven hundred and fifty miles, which might be traversed by a steamer in less than three days. If, at any future time, a railway were carried along the Mekran coast, this part of the journey would be further accelerated. But taking Bunder Abbas as the terminus, we have the whole time, from the British capital to the nearest Indian port, about ten days and a half, instead of thirty, the time now occupied by the route through Egypt.

In comparing, however, the merits of the several schemes for a railway to the Persian Gulf, it will be apparent that one of the chief advantages which that of Sir Macdonald Stephenson possesses is, that it will, no doubt, soon have its first great station, from Calais to the Bosphorus, completed by the construction of the Roumelian lines. This is an advantage which, though originally looked forward to by Sir Macdonald, his scheme had not, when first projected, but which now, unquestionably, gives it an enormous superiority over Mr. Andrew's proposed route; as the break in the latter, between the Italian coast of the Adriatic and Suedia, is an objection that is impossible to be overcome. The line proper, therefore, from Scutari, starting with this advantage, will have a certainty of enormous through traffic already secured to it. This, it is true, may also, as far as Brindisi, be claimed for Mr. Andrew's scheme, but from that port to the Gulf, this latter—with the exception of the short run through Northern Syria—would be almost entirely dependent on the direct traffic *alone* for its support; seeing that little or nothing could be expected from the long stretch of desert to be traversed from Ja'ber Castle to Bussorah. Not so, however, with Sir Macdonald Stephenson's proposed route through Asia Minor; as from Scutari to Alexandretta, and thence to Aleppo, it would run through populous and well-cultivated districts, with a large traffic at once available, and which would be speedily and enormously increased by the transport facilities afforded by such a line.

The dividend-paying value of this traffic would, of course, depend on the cost of the railway, but a reliable estimate of the expense of its construction states the average, at the outside, at not more than the sum I have mentioned—£12,000 to £15,000 a mile. The success, too, of the Smyrna and Cassaba Railway, justifies the belief that a large and profitable local traffic would speedily become available, seeing that, although the Cassaba Railway begins at an important port, it may be said to end nowhere; whereas the Trans-Asia Minor line would run through and connect all the most important industrial and producing districts between the Bosphorus and the Euphrates. For example, the principal north road, which starts from Alexandretta through Asia Minor, forms a junction at Kutahia with the roads from Brussa and Angora, and, continuing thence in a still northerly direction to Ismidt, skirts the north-eastern shore of the Sea of Marmora to Scutari on the Bosphorus. From Smyrna, the main road passes through Ali-Shehr to Sandukli and Afiun Kara-Hissar, whence it branches, in a north and north-easterly direction, to Ismidt and Angora, and south-easterly to Konieh and the Syrian frontier. These districts, too, are well-watered by the Kasalmack, the Kizel-Irmak, the Sakaria, the Sarabat, and the Bojuk-Meinder, which are all, more or less, adapted for canalization, and would, by such means, become feeders for a railway running from Scutari to Alexandretta. Such a line, therefore, as proposed by Sir Macdonald Stephenson, passing by Ismidt, Kutahia, Afiun Kara-Hissar, Konieh, Ak-Seraï, Yeni-Shehr, and Kaiseria, would connect important centres of population, and speedily attract to itself the goods traffic of the great opium, silk, wool, grain, and oil-producing districts of Anatolia.

Once arrived at Alexandretta, Sir Macdonald Stephenson's scheme, in common with that of Mr. Latham, would possess the great advantage over Mr. Andrew's line of pursuing the long-established caravan route followed now, and for centuries past, by the local transport trade, as well as by that between the Mediterranean and the Trans-Euphrates countries. Thus, by taking this track instead of that from Suedia, the line would immediately command a large traffic, as, although the distance between Aleppo and Alexandretta is only sixty miles, the present cost of conveying goods for shipment is £6 per ton, and the carriage of wheat, 17s. 6d. per quarter, or double the price of the grain itself. From Aleppo, however, Sir Macdonald's route, as I understand it, joins that proposed by Mr. Andrew, and shares the disadvantages of the latter by striking the Euphrates at Ja'ber Castle, and thence following the desert river valley down south to Kurnah, instead of adhering to the old-established track over the Euphrates at Birejik, and thence, across Northern Mesopotamia, through a populous and productive country, and past the thriving towns of Orfa—further fed by a tramway or short branch to Diarbekhr—Mardin, Nisibin, Jezireh, Zakho, Mosul, and Bagdad.

Nearly the whole of this country is rich in oil, wheat, barley, maize, rice, tobacco, madder-root, wool, mohair, silk, tallow, fruits, honey, cotton, galls, orpiment, wax, and gums; but although a large trade at present exists, it is as nothing compared with what it might become if more rapid means of communication were once established between the interior and the coast. It has been, in fact, calculated that if only one-half of the surface of Mesopotamia were put under cultivation, it would yield grain equal to the produce of the whole of France; and that, if conveyed to Alexandretta by rail, ample supplies could be sold in London at the same price, if not cheaper than that brought from Odessa, with the advantage of its arriving periodically in the early spring, when the price of wheat is usually on the rise in Western markets.* Up to the very slopes of the Kurdish mountains the soil teems with fertility; and a settled and industrious population would not merely afford cheap and abundant labour for the construction of the railway, but, at the same time, provide an amount of protection and local traffic which could by no means be obtained on the route by Ja'ber Castle. Besides, the towns I have enumerated, as well as the many smaller ones which border on this great caravan route, would supply the elements of safety and success to an extent such as Annah, Semlum, Hillah, and the other far-between Arab hamlets on the Euphrates would be totally unable to furnish. It

---

* In ancient times, Mesopotamia was so admirably adapted for the cultivation of corn that it seldom produced less than from two hundred to three hundred fold. "The ear of the wheat as well as the barley," says Herodotus, "is four digits broad, but the immense height to which the cenchrus and sesamum stalks grow, although I have witnessed it myself, I dare not mention, lest those who have not visited the country should disbelieve my report."

is true, as already stated, that this route is longer by about two hundred miles than that by the Euphrates, but the former possesses advantages which would much more than compensate for any expense occasioned by the *détour* north-eastwards. The trifling increased difference would continue to the line from Aleppo to the Gulf all the advantages of a local traffic scarcely, if at all, inferior to that which might be hoped for from Asia Minor—a consideration, it need scarcely be said, which would give this section an immense economical superiority over the Euphrates Valley route, without losing a passenger or a ton of the through traffic between Europe and India.

It is, therefore, not an unreasonable expectation that the lowest traffic would, within a year or two after the opening of the line, pay four or five per cent. on the expenditure; nor is it extravagant to suppose that this would be increased by the passenger and through traffic, so that, in a very few years, the earnings would amply cover any guarantee that might be undertaken by our Government. The traffic between India and Europe is showing a disposition to return to its more direct and natural course; and I believe that the proposed scheme of a railway from Scutari to the Gulf, with the modification I have mentioned from Aleppo, possesses all the elements, not merely of engineering practicability at a moderate cost, but of great subsequent commercial success. The solution of this railway problem, and the order of it, I consider, then, to be—the construction, first, of the Tigris Valley line from Alexandretta *via* Aleppo; striking the Euphrates at Birejik, and past the towns of Orfa, Mardin, Nisibin, Mosul, and Bagdad to the Gulf at Kurnah or Bussorah. The line would thus run through one of the richest alluvial valleys in the world, which, with such an outlet for its teeming produce, would soon become a chief granary of Europe, and a cotton field rivalling India itself. In fact, to those who know the country, the advantages of the Tigris over the Euphrates route, in every respect, except distance, simply admit of no discussion. To complete the link, however, between the English Channel and the Persian Gulf, Sir Macdonald Stephenson's Trans-Asia Minor line, from Scutari to Alexandretta, should be subsequently constructed.

CHAPTER XIV.

BEYROUT TO CYPRUS.

The traveller who has been fortunate enough to pass the spring in Syria will do well to take Cyprus, Smyrna, and Constantinople on his way home. The Austrian Lloyd's steamers, as well as those of the French Messageries Maritimes, leave Beyrout every week for Smyrna; but I prefer the former, as they call *en route* at Cyprus, Rhodes, and Scio.

On arriving early in the morning at Larnaca, the ancient Citium, now the chief port of Cyprus, sufficient time is allowed to go on shore, and inspect everything worth seeing. The streets are clean, and the interior of the houses—mostly only one storey high above the ground floor—is very comfortable; the apartments being generally paved with white marble, and the houses themselves surrounded by pretty gardens, in which the Cypriotes take great pleasure. Larnaca is the residence of the European Consuls, and carries on a considerable trade; but it is strange its roadstead should be preferred to the old port of Famagûsta, which offers the advantages of a safe and commodious harbour. If the marshes in the vicinity of the latter were drained, the harbour cleared, and the old works to seaward reconstructed, Cyprus would possess one of the finest harbours in the Levant. Before the Turkish occupation, Cyprus contained upwards of 1,000,000 inhabitants; but it is now estimated there are not more than 180,000, distributed amongst 605 towns and villages, of which 118 are exclusively inhabited by Mussulmans, 248 by Christians, and 239 by Moslems and Christians. As a consequence of the diminished population of Cyprus, an immense breadth of land is lying waste and uncultivated; but if the population were sufficiently increased, and the soil were properly tilled, it would be difficult to estimate the future agricultural produce of the country. This island was formerly the granary of the Levant. It produces wheat, barley, silk, cotton, wool, madder, flax, sesame, tobacco, colocinth, oil, wine, figs, currants, honey, &c., and it is known that rich mines of sulphur, coal, copper, and iron exist. Pliny tells us that, in his time, the wealth of Cyprus arose, to a considerable extent, from its copper mines, the most productive of which were those of Tamassus, in the centre of the island; Soli, on the north coast; and Amathos and Cyrium, on the south. Gold and silver were also found; while the precious stones of Cyprus—the diamond, emerald, agate, malachite, opal, and jaspar—were held in high estimation by the Romans. No one, however, possessing sufficient scientific knowledge of the subject has recently explored Cyprus in search of minerals, although the entire character of the island promises most satisfactory results. There is probably no place where living has been hitherto so easy as at Cyprus; even the beggars — who are mostly blind, maimed, or worn out by age, and have generally a small house of their own—are able to live quietly at home, without begging more than one or two days a week. The island, too, has generally had the reputation of being one of the healthiest in the Mediterranean, although recent experience would rather indicate the contrary.

I am nevertheless inclined to believe that it is not so much the climate as imprudence which has caused the amount of sickness lately prevailing at Cyprus. No one accustomed to the East would think of travelling during the great heat of the day, and the culpability of marching troops under an August and September sun can hardly be excused. Lower Egypt, from my own experience, is very healthy, with proper precautions, but if the same imprudence were committed there, dysentery would inevitably ensue; in Syria, intermittent fever would be the consequence, and so it has been in Cyprus. The troops should have commenced their march an hour before sunrise, rested during the great heat of the day, avoiding all stimulants, and resumed their march two hours before sunset. Had this been done, I am convinced that much of the sickness prevailing among our troops in Cyprus would have been avoided. Another mistake that has been made was in sending the men immediately to hospital; and, as practice is better than theory, I shall give a case in point. Travelling once in Syria, I committed the imprudence of remaining for several hours under the mid-day sun, and, on arriving at Beyrout, I felt exceedingly ill with all the premonitory symptoms of intermittent fever. Instead, however, of going to the doctor, I went to the Turkish bath, and two hours' sweating killed the fever. Now, at Cyprus, our troops, in the first instance, ought not to have been marched during the heat of the mid-day sun, and, in the second, instead of being sent at once to hospital, they should have been sent to the bath. Occasional doses of quinine, judicious use of the Turkish bath, and protection from the mid-day sun, are the best preventives of intermittent fever in the East.

No preparations had, strange to say, been made for the reception of our troops, and, without barracks or buildings of any kind, they were obliged to bivouac in a manner most prejudicial to their health. In a climate so hot during August and September, and in a country so ill-drained as Cyprus ordinary tents are comparatively useless, and the construction of buildings should be entrusted to those who are familiar with the climatic conditions of the island. If our Government had had the ordinary foresight of consulting a native mercantile firm, all the necessary accommodation could have been completed in time so as to have avoided the fiasco which has brought so much discredit on England. There was no difficulty in finding such a firm, for instance, that of Bustros is not only known throughout every port in the Levant, but enjoys a reputation second to none other in Europe. The Bustros family is one of the oldest in Syria; and their wealth, popularity, and recognized position place them beyond the temptations which firms less fortunately situated might possibly be unable to resist in executing contracts for our Government. They have establishments in Beyrout, Alexandria, Cyprus, and London, the latter of which is represented by a member of the firm who has become an Englishman by naturalization. At the present moment, I learn that an English sanatorium is contemplated at the village of Allay in Mount Lebanon, about two hours' distance from Beyrout, and there, as well as in other parts of Syria and Cyprus, the Bustros' family possess large estates. The Viceroy of Egypt, and several foreign Princes, have been guests under their hospitable roof at Beyrout; and, from my own personal knowledge of the house of Bustros, extending over twenty years, I feel I am doing a service to the English Government in suggesting the advisability of seeking the co-operation of such a firm in the construction of any public works that may be undertaking in either Cyprus or Mount Lebanon.

CHAPTER XV.

CYPRUS.*

The island of Cyprus is separated from the coast of Karamania by a channel of about twenty-five leagues in width. Its area approximates to 1000 square leagues, which may be subdivided in the following manner:—one-fifth, having a mountainous character, is adapted for the growth of timber; but a portion could be turned to account for the culture of the vine. This mountainous district of the island offers immense resources; the forests of Thrados alone, which lie in this section, would, if properly managed, produce annually a considerable number of pine trees. Oaks are also seen in

* This chapter is reproduced from my book, "The Resources of Turkey," which is now out of print. As it was written at a time when there was no idea of the British acquisition of Cyprus, the particulars given may not be devoid of interest.

thousands on the declivities, that extend, for five leagues, close to the sea. Two-fifths of the island are occupied by hills, on which grow, chiefly, olives, mulberries, vines, and fruit-trees of all sorts. The remaining two-fifths are composed of magnificent plains and extensive open country, which, though wanting in rivers and streams, are still very productive in cereals; in fact, the eastern portion has always been the granary of the island.

Soil.—The soil of Cyprus is of very great fertility, and formerly supplied the wants of a population of upwards of a million: it still kindly responds to the natural indolence and want of skill of its inhabitants, of whom hardly one-fourth are devoted to agriculture.

Agriculture.—Labourers use a kind of plough, a rude and miserable implement, without wheels, drawn by two oxen, and driven by one man; like the earliest plough, it scarcely penetrates the soil more than two inches. It is used in the tillage of the plains, and the cultivation of the vineyards and vegetable gardens. The husbandmen generally wait until the autumnal rains have softened the soil, and then, after ploughing up twice, they sow the seed, and merely level the earth with a common plank.

Any young man, though far from able-bodied, can drive one of these ploughs, sow, and, with the aid of the women, reap and stow the produce. The few districts in the island which have the advantage of running water are chiefly devoted to the culture of cotton, barley, and wheat; sesame and vegetables are but little cultivated. The water is, at stated times, distributed over the different meadows, but, as these are not well levelled, the earth is unequally moistened, and the water frequently sinks away without rendering any service.

Products.—The island produces cereals in abundance, wool, cotton, madder, silk, flax, sesame, tobacco, colocinth, oil, wine, figs, currants, oranges, honey, pitch, skins; yellow, red, and green umber; butter, and cheese. These products, which have been more abundant in later than in preceding years, will continue to increase with the importance acquired by the agricultural population, as immense tracts of waste land exist that might be profitably cultivated for every purpose. The cultivation especially of the vine and mulberry would be followed by satisfactory results. The silk-worm of Cyprus furnishes two harvests in one year; the first generation produces the cocoon in the early part of April, lays eggs, revives, and in thus reviving spins a second cocoon about the end of May. This has often been confirmed by experiments. The silk harvest of Cyprus will always be in proportion to the number of hands engaged in that branch of industry; mulberry-trees flourish, and the silkworm sheds may be erected in the open air.

Mineral Products.—The mineral products of the island have hitherto been unexplored; it is, however, certain that many mines would be discovered of sulphur, coal, copper, iron, and perhaps also of gold and silver. Tradition and romance speak much of treasures concealed in the island of Cyprus. No one, however, has yet explored the island who was cognizant of these matters; but, in the neighbourhood of Cape Blanc, sulphur may be seen on the surface of the soil, and the entire character of the island promises most satisfactory results to those who would develop its mineral productions.

Salt-pits, &c.—Cyprus possesses two rich natural salt-pits, one of which is situated half a league from Larnaca, and the other a third of a league from Limassol. There are also coloured earths, trees, and roots adapted for dyeing; pot-herbs grow wild in the fields and prairies, while on the hills there are rich pasturages, which would feed numerous flocks.

Manufactures.—At Cyprus, the arts and trades remain stationary; machinery and other contrivances for simplifying work and saving hand labour are quite unknown. At Nicosia, Larnaca, Killani, and some other places, silk tissues for home consumption are prepared, which are good and solid, but of coarse execution. Woollen slippers are also made, especially the red and yellow ones used by the Turks. Besides these, there are manufactured,—lace, stuffs, and other articles; but the production is hardly adequate to the demand, and there is, consequently, a large field for speculation in various manufactures, metals, tools, &c.

Ports.—Larnaca, the residence of the European consuls, is the chief sea-port of the island. Ships of war, steamers, and sailing vessels coming to Cyprus, usually cast anchor in the roadstead, which is formed by the two capes of Pilla and of Kitti, and affords a tolerable anchorage. Through Larnaca pass all the manufactured goods imported, as well as almost all the cereals, and a considerable part of the wines, caroubs, and silks exported from the island. The population amounts to 15,000, of whom a third are Turks.

Limassol is the chief port for the wine and bean trades, and has acquired considerable importance within the past few years on account of the demand for wines and spirits. It would be difficult to calculate the possible produce of Cyprus if the island contained a million of agriculturists, for the entire place is one unworked mine of enormous wealth. The hills alone which surround Limassol might produce annually, to an almost unlimited extent, the currants so highly prized in Europe; and, although there is not a single vine in a circuit of more than four leagues from the town, Limassol, nevertheless, exports a million barrels of wine as the produce of the mountains of the province, of which hardly one-tenth is cultivated. The olive and caroub trees grow together on the chain of mountains encircling Limassol, without any cultivation being bestowed on them, while the hills are covered in some places with oaks planted in the time of the Venetians. Limassol contains between 5000 and 6000 inhabitants, of whom one-third are Turks.

Famagûsta, so famous under the Venetians, possesses an excellent spacious port, which, however, is now so choked up with mud that it can only hold about a dozen small craft. It is well sheltered from all winds, and, if deepened, which could be done at a small expense, would contain hundreds of large ships.

Roads.—The roads are rather better in Cyprus than in most other parts of the Ottoman Empire, but they still fall far short of the requirements of the island. From Nicosia, which is centrally situated, roads, varying in importance from bridle paths to bullock tracks, radiate to different parts of the island—one going through Larnaca, Limassol, and Famagûsta. A good road, however, from the capital to Larnaca is much needed, and before any important expansion of trade can take place, the whole of the roads will require to be substantially improved. At present, with only a small proportion of the arable area under cultivation, even the existing roads are quite inadequate. If the agricultural and mineral resources of Cyprus were but fairly developed, the island would yield a revenue which would justify a large expenditure on works of public improvement.

Commerce.—The products of the island, such as cotton, silk, madder, wool, lambskins, wheat, barley, commanderie wine, caroubs, linseed, colocinth, sesame, and currants, are exported to France, England, Trieste, Malta, the Ionian Islands, Leghorn, Genoa, and Venice; the other products are exported to Alexandria, Constantinople, Smyrna, Syria, and the islands of the Archipelago. To France is sent all the silk, and a large portion of the cotton, madder, wool, sesame, and flax-seed. To England, cereals, and madder. To Trieste and Venice, commanderie wine, cottons, madders, beans, flax-seed, colocinth, lamb-skins, sesame, and currants. To Leghorn, commanderie wine, wool, cotton, madder, and cereals. To Constantinople, Alexandria, Smyrna, Syria, Karamania, and the isles of the Archipelago, common wines, brandy, spirits of wine, beans, cereals, pitch, tar, cheese, onions, and vinegar. The present prices of produce sold free on board, including every expense, are as follow:—

Cotton	per oke of 2¾ lbs.	7½	piastres.
Madder	,, ,,	6	,,
Wool	,, ,,	6	,,
Silk	,, ,,	250	,,
Flax seed	,, ,,	2¼	,,
Sesame	,, ,,	3	,,
Colocinth	,, ,,	10	,,
Currants	,, ,,	2½	,,
Commanderie wine	,, ,,	3	,,
Common wine	,, ,,	2	,,
Brandy	,, ,,	6	,,
Spirits of wine	,, ,,	34	,,
Vinegar	,, ,,	1	,,
Beans	per kintal	40	,,
Wheat	per kilo	30	,,
Barley	,,	15	,,

The imports are limited to the mere necessaries of local consumption. Formerly, Cyprus furnished to the neighbouring coasts of Syria and Karamania the articles which she now imports. These are sugars, coffee, leather, cotton yarn, copper boilers and saucepans, iron, steel, paper, glass, small shot, fowling-pieces, woollen cloths, silks, rice, soap, candles, vitriol, alum, logwood, sal-ammoniac, cod-fish, sardines, eels, indigo, boards, &c. All cotton goods and indigo come from England. France furnishes colonial produce, leather, woollen cloth, small shot, silk stuffs, gums, and cod-fish. Trieste contributes glass, steel, iron, nails, wrought copper, paper, wax, candles, boards, and sardines. Rice comes from Egypt; soap and eels from Syria.*

Population.—In the time of the Venetians, the population of Cyprus was upwards of 1,000,000. In 1840, the entire population of the island was only 100,000; it is now, however, calculated at 180,000. The number of Turkish families is 7299, and of Christian families 19,215, making a total of 26,514 families.

Condition of the Inhabitants.—Those inactive masses who live from hand to mouth are not to be found in Cyprus; all who wish for employ-

---

* See "Trade of Cyprus." Appendix IV.

ment can obtain it. The want of hands is so much felt that any one, having a distaste for the calling of fisherman or boatman, can find employment at once as cooper, porter, wine-gauger, broker for foreign captains, &c. The country enjoys perfect tranquillity; thefts are very rare, and robberies are unknown. Many years have passed since an assassination occurred in the island; and altogether Cyprus enjoys the reputation of being the most peaceable island in the Mediterranean. Its present state is that of a country which once was celebrated, rich, and populous; which now is but the shadow of its former days, but for which a better destiny may be reserved.

CHAPTER XVI.

CYPRUS TO CONSTANTINOPLE.

Leaving Cyprus in the afternoon, the steamer arrives next morning at Rhodes, which is interesting on account of its classical associations, as well as from its having been the home, in more recent times, of the brave Knights of St. John. There can be no doubt that vast treasures of art lie buried in Rhodes; for, besides the famed Colossus, three thousand other statues adorned the ancient city, one hundred of which were of such a size that, Pliny says, the possession of one of them would be sufficient to make any place celebrated. The temples were also full of the finest paintings, the masterpieces of Protogenes, Zeuxis, and other artists of the Rhodian School. Homer, besides, speaks of three Doric cities in the island—Lindus, Camirus, and Jalyssus—that flourished long before the city of Rhodes was founded, and in which were several magnificent temples erected in honour of Hercules and Minerva. The sites of those ancient cities are now marked by the town of Lindos, and the villages of Camiro and Jaliso. For upwards of two hundred years the Knights of St. John held Rhodes against the attacks of the Turks, until at length, in 1522, the Grand Master, Villiers de Lisle Adam, capitulated to Solyman "the Magnificent," and retired with his companions to the island of Malta. The remains of the fortifications erected by the Knights are interesting specimens of the military architecture of the middle ages, but the Church of St. John has long since been converted into a mosque, and the hospitals, as well as the palace of the Grand Master, are now in ruins. The streets of the town are rather gloomy, the street of the Knights Templars being the only one that may be considered straight and well paved.

From Rhodes the steamer takes its course in sight of Patmos, celebrated as the place where St. John wrote his revelations; Cos, the birthplace of Apelles, Hippocrates, and Ptolemy Philadelphus; then by Samos, the birthplace of Pythagoras, to Scio, the ancient Chios, which it reaches at early dawn. Scio is celebrated for its excellent wine, salubrious climate, and beautiful women. It was treated with especial favour by the Turks, as it enjoyed the protection of the Sultana Validé, and, before the Greek revolution of 1822, was represented to be a garden inhabited by a happy and contented people. The Sciotes were unfortunately induced to take part in the insurrection by some turbulent or piratical Greeks from Samos and Candia, and, on the arrival of the Capitan Pasha with a large force, were put to the sword with great slaughter. Before the revolution, the population of the island amounted to more than 120,000 souls, but in the year 1830 the number was scarcely 20,000. As the births, however, are in excess of the deaths, in consequence of the healthiness of the climate, the population has sensibly increased, and is now estimated at 70,000. Scio is one of the most beautiful islands in the Archipelago; its scenery is varied and charming, and its inhabitants are enterprising and intelligent. A large proportion of the commercial establishments in Turkey are owned by natives of the island, and the richest Greek merchants in England have nearly all come from Scio.

Smyrna, formerly called the "Crown of Ionia," and "Gem of Asia," is reached at 10 or 11 A.M.

It is delightfully situated at the extremity of a gulf about thirty miles in length, and varying from five to fifteen miles in breadth, encompassed with high mountains which are in many parts richly wooded. Seen from the harbour, the appearance of the town, extending two miles along the coast, and rising from the sea in the form of an amphitheatre, is very striking; the houses in the Frank and Armenian quarters are well built of stone, and the streets, although narrow, are superior to those of Constantinople. Seven cities, it is said, disputed the right of having given birth to Homer, but Smyrna claims that honour, and tradition asserts that he composed his immortal poems in a grotto on the bank of the river Melés, which runs at a little distance to the south of the city. There are several very good hotels in Smyrna, and also in the pleasant villages of Bournabat and Boudja, to which there are now branch lines of railway. The latter is a charming residence in summer, and is only five and a half miles by the Smyrna and Aidin Railway, which has a short branch of a mile and a half to the village from Paradise station. Smyrna enjoys the distinction of being the only place in Turkey, with the exception of Stamboul, containing the termini of two railways, one to Cassaba and the other to Aidin. Near the station of Magnésie, on the former line, two and a half hours' journey, there is a remarkable statue of Niobe, supposed to be the work of Proteus, son of Tantalus, and of which Pausanius and Strabo speak. The ruins of Ephesus, too, are now particularly well worth a visit, in consequence of the excavations that have been carried on by Dr. Wood upon the site of the great Temple of Diana. The distance by the Smyrna and Aidin Railway to Ayasoulouk is forty-eight miles; time, two hours fifty minutes; horses can there be hired for Ephesus, and the return journey to Smyrna made the same day. Special trains may be had on moderate terms at short notice, and parties of twelve or more can obtain return tickets at the rate of a single fare by giving one day's notice to the station-master at Smyrna.

The society of Smyrna is very agreeable, and the principal nationalities have each their own club, at which balls are frequently given; in fact, Smyrna has the character of being the most hospitable city in the Levant. There is an excellent theatre, and also several cafés at which entertainments are occasionally produced, and where, during the heat of the day, the refreshing sea-breeze may be enjoyed with a cup of fragrant mocha and a cool narghilé. A fearful accident occurred some time ago during the performance at one of these cafés, known as the Kivoto. Attracted by handbills posted all over the town, upwards of two hundred and fifty spectators flocked to the exhibition, but about 10 P.M. an ominous cracking was heard, and the horrified audience felt the flooring give way beneath them. A single piercing shriek of anguish was heard to issue from the café, followed by a loud crash, and all was silent. The entire edifice, which was built over the sea and supported on piles, had disappeared under the water, a few shattered beams alone remaining to indicate the spot where the Kivoto stood. Upwards of one hundred persons perished, among them being all the actors and actresses with the exception of the clown. It was a strange coincidence that at the very moment of the catastrophe one of the performers was representing Death, and caused much laughter by running after another actor on the stage. The climate of Smyrna is considered to be healthy; even in the month of August I did not find the heat excessive, as, during the summer, a breeze, called the "Inbat," blows from the sea, and keeps the town cool and pleasant. When, however, the wind comes from the north, which it occasionally does, across the hot plains of Anatolia, the air is oppressive; but in the months of May and June the climate is very agreeable.

Steamers leave Smyrna several times a week for Constantinople, calling at Mitylene—the ancient Lesbos, Tenedos, the Dardanelles, and Gallipoli. The Troad is now more than ever interesting to archæologists on account of the excavations commenced by Mr. Frank Calvert of the Dardanelles, and continued by Mr. A. Schliemann, with a view to settle the long-disputed question of the site of Troy; the former being of opinion that if Homeric Troy ever existed, the probability is the place now called Hissarlik marks the spot where it stood.

CHAPTER XVII.

SUMMER ON THE BOSPHORUS.

For excellence of situation, Constantinople—the ancient Byzantium—is not excelled by any other city in the world. The first view on rounding Seraglio Point, as the morning breaks in calm beauty over the Anatolian hills, and the sun tips with gold the countless minarets of Stamboul, is, perhaps, one of the most exquisite in the world. On one side, the glorious Bosphorus; on the other, the Sea of Marmora; in the far distance, the mountains of Bithynia, and the snow-crowned summit of Mount Olympus; in front, Scutari, the ancient Chrysopolis, with its melancholy-looking cypress groves; then Kadikeui, the ancient Chalcedon; and nearer, the beautiful panorama from Seraglio Point, past the Sublime Porte, the mosques of Saint Sophia, of Sultans Achmet, Bajaset, Soleyman, and Mahmoud, the tower of the Seraskeriat, the ruined aqueduct to Eyoub, and the dark cypresses of "the place of a thousand tombs." It is a charming scene, and the remembrance of its beauty remains for ever on the mind like a dream that cannot be forgotten. To see Constantinople, it used to be said that you should enter the Golden Horn from the Sea of Marmora, steam up the Bosphorus, and out by the Black Sea, as when you once placed your foot on shore at Galata the illusion vanished. In justice, however, it must be admitted that so many improvements have recently been made in Stamboul, especially when Server Pasha was Prefect, that this remark is no longer applicable to the same extent. The streets of Galata, it is true, will not bear comparison with Oxford Street or Cheapside, and the pavement of the Grand' Rue de Pera is not conducive to equanimity of temper; but these little inconveniences are soon forgotten when contemplating the matchless scenery of the Bosphorus, or when comfortably housed under the hospitable roof of the Hôtel d'Angleterre, or the Hôtel Byzance. Missirie, unhappily, does not rule at the former as of old, and I should now give the preference to the latter. At the Hôtel Byzance, in the Grand' Rue, the traveller will enjoy all the novelty of the East, with the ease, comfort, and cleanliness of the West.

Constantinople, like Rome, was built on seven hills, and this is the chief cause, not only of its picturesque appearance, but of the healthiness of its climate, receiving as it does all the breezes from the Sea of Marmora, the Euxine, and the adjoining plains of Thrace. The two principal suburbs, Galata and Pera, are on the opposite side of the Golden Horn—connected with Stamboul by a floating wooden bridge—the former being the commercial centre, and the latter the place of residence of the Christian population. Byzantium was founded in 658 B.C., by Byzas, King of Megara. Having left Greece with the intention of building a new city, he consulted the oracle of Apollo on the subject, and Strabo states that Phythia advised him to erect it opposite to the city of the blind. This, Byzas subsequently discovered, or rather conjectured, to mean Chalcedon (now Kadikeui), whose inhabitants were foolish enough not to have seen the superior advantages which the opposite coast offered for a settlement. During nearly a thousand years Byzantium suffered many vicissitudes of fortune, until, in A.D. 330, Constantine made it the capital of the Eastern empire, and enriched it with treasures of art taken from all parts of the Roman world. In the time of Justinian, A.D. 527 to 565, this Eastern empire comprised Dacia, Macedonia, and the East proper, in Europe; the Hellespont, the islands, Anatolia, Armenia, Mesopotamia, Syria, Palestine, and the provinces bathed by the Euxine, in Asia; the entire of Egypt, Numidia, Mauritania, and four provinces of Carthage, in Africa, together with Lusitania and Italy. In the reign of Constantine XIII., however, the empire consisted only of the city of Constantinople itself, with about twenty towns and the districts of the Morea; and when the last of the Palæologi fell in defence of his capital before the conquering arms of the son of Amurath, it was no wonder he exclaimed, Θέλω θάνειν μᾶλλον ἡ ξῆν—"I had rather die than live!"

It is generally supposed that when Mohammed II. took possession of Constantinople, he planted the "Crescent and the Star" for the first time upon its walls. But the crescent was, in fact, the ancient emblem of Byzantine power. Philip of Macedon, who had long desired to get possession of the city, took advantage of a dark night to surprise it, and his soldiers had almost gained the walls when the dogs, which were kept for the purpose of warning the sentinels against night attacks, made such a noise by their unusual barking that the Byzantines, advised of danger, flocked to the rescue. Darkness, however, prevented them from acting until, suddenly, the moon became unveiled, and brightened up the exterior of the city. The Macedonians were repulsed, and, in gratitude, the Byzantines chose the goddess Hecate as their tutelary divinity, and represented her under the form of a crescent and a star. Constantine the Great adopted this emblem when he transferred the seat of his empire to Byzantium, and the Ottomans have since maintained it. The name of Byzantium was, in A.D. 330, changed to that of Constantinopolis, or city of Constantine. It was spoken of by the Greeks as Πόλις in the same manner as the Romans styled Rome, Urbs; and a slight alteration of the words Εἰς τὴν πόλιν is supposed to have produced the name of Istamboul, or Stamboul, by which the city, as distinguished from the suburbs, is now called by the Turks.

In some respects, Constantinople is pleasanter in winter than in summer, as, in winter, the theatres, opera, and other places of amusement are open, and balls are frequently given by the various foreign embassies in Pera, as well as by the rich Greek and Armenian bankers of Galata. For those, however, who visit the Bosphorus in search of health, or seek a delightful climate and beautiful scenery, the months of May, June, and July are far more preferable. The sun shines brightly every day, but the heat is never excessive, as the Etesian, or north wind, blows constantly from the Black Sea, and keeps the temperature always moderate. I cannot imagine anything in nature more lovely than the Bosphorus:

> "The European with the Asian shore
>   Sprinkled with palaces; the ocean stream
> Here and there studded with a seventy-four;
>   Sophia's cupola with golden gleam;
> The cypress groves; Olympus high and hoar;
>   The twelve isles, and the more than I could dream,
> Far less describe."

In May, most persons migrate from Pera and Stamboul to the Prince's Islands in the Sea of Marmora, or to the numerous villages between the Golden Horn and the Black Sea. Kandili, on the Asiatic shore, is considered to be the healthiest village on the Bosphorus, but Therapia and Buyukderé are the most fashionable; the palaces of the English and French embassies being at the former, and that of Russia at the latter. In fact, both sides of the Bosphorus are thickly studded with the handsome villas of the Galata bankers, and the palaces of the Sultan and his ministers.

It would be difficult to say which of the Sultan's palaces is the most magnificent, for each has some beauty special to itself. The Palace of Dolma-Baghtché is the palace *par excellence;* but the Kiosk at the Sweet Waters of Asia, although small, is particularly chaste and striking in its exterior appearance, while the interior of that at Beylerbey is well worth inspection. This palace, on the Asiatic shore, is situated upon one of the most beautiful of the many beautiful spots on the banks of the Bosphorus. Close to the water, it is on three sides enclosed by a curtain of verdure which extends over the slopes of the rising hills that form the foot of Mount Barougourlu; and the interior displays all that luxury and magnificence with which Oriental monarchs love to surround themselves. Prodigies of Moorish decoration meet the eye everywhere; the ceilings and walls are inlaid with gold, and fantastic designs in thousands of colours, blending harmoniously together; hangings of golden tissue in various patterns fall round the windows and before the doors; while the choicest furniture, the *chefs-d'œuvre* of Sèvres, and the extraordinary productions of China and Japan add to the general effect. The principal entrance is from the south, overlooking the garden, whence a rich staircase of a double spiral form leads to the grand drawing-room, or *salle d'honneur*. On the left, there is a large room *à coupole;* and on the right, at the side next the Bosphorus, is the throne-room, in the Moorish style, and altogether in marqueterie, at the end of which are large niches supported by columns of rare woods encrusted with ornaments in ivory of most exquisite delicacy. An ornamentation of the same kind decorates the different panels forming the basement and spaces between the niches; while a frieze, composed of a series of small columns, divided by festoons in mosaic, runs round the upper part of the cornice. At the bottom of this room, raised some height from the floor, is placed the throne, resplendent in gold and precious stones. From the apartments you enter the grand drawing-room, round which runs a colonnade; splendid lustres hang from the ceiling; candelabra of exquisite workmanship are attached to each column; Persian carpets cover the floor; Turkish divans of brocade or embroidered velvet are relieved by sofas of European fashion; magnificent pier glasses adorn the walls; the whole combining Western comfort with Eastern display. This saloon gives access to the bath-room, in which there are three compartments. The first is called the *frigidarium;* thence you enter the *tepidarium*, which is moderately heated, and then into the third apartment, or *calidarium*, where the temperature is at its highest point. The bath-room proper—that is, the *tepidarium* and *calidarium*—is composed of pure white marble, the ceilings being formed in the shape of a dome, through which the light is admitted in such a subdued and singular manner that the vault has the appearance of being filled with some translucid substance. The gardens of the palace, perhaps the most wonderful of the whole as a work of art, are disposed in terraces rising one above the other to a great height, each filled with the choicest flowers. On the topmost of these terraces a miniature lake has been formed, ornamented with grottoes, and shaded by the parasol pine, magnolias, willows, and various trees and shrubs that give forth a delicious perfume. The view, when seated in one of the caïques on this lake, particularly at sunset, is most illusive and extraordinary; for, as nothing is seen beyond but the summits of the hills, the pellucid atmosphere above, and the golden sky in the distance, you can almost imagine yourself following the sun, suspended in the midst of the air.

Although, as I have already said, summer is the non-season at Constantinople, there are plenty of amusements suitable to the time of year. Steamers ply all day up and down the Bosphorus, as well as to Prinkipo and other islands in the Sea of Marmora, while numerous caïques wait for hire at every landing-place. In the evenings the esplanade at Buyukderé is crowded with promenaders, and the full-dress toilettes of the Perote ladies give an idea of an *al-fresco* ball. Music and fireworks enliven the scene, and when, on some special occasion, both sides of the Bosphorus are illuminated, the whole appears rather like a dream of fairyland than a reality of every-day life. On the anniversary of the Sultan's accession to the throne, a splendid entertainment is usually given by the Grand Vizier, to which, with a little influence, invitations may be obtained. Owing to the late war, however, this has for the present been discontinued. Then there are the " Sweet Waters of Asia," and " Sweet Waters of Europe "—the beauties of which have been so frequently described—where the Turkish ladies drive in their little gilt carriages on Fridays; Scutari, with its dark cypresses, and burial-place of the English brave who fell during the Crimean War; the forest of Belgrade; the "Giant's Mountain," much frequented by holiday parties, and from which there is a fine view up the Euxine:

> " 'Tis a grand sight, from off the Giant's grave,
> To watch the progress of those rolling seas
> Between the Bosphorus, as they lash and lave
> Europe and Asia, you being quite at ease."

These, and numerous other places in the neighbourhood, will afford ample pleasure and amusement during a couple of months' residence in the "City of the Sultan." Besides the steamers and caïques, there is now another mode of locomotion —namely, the railway, of which there are two lines running some distance from Stamboul.

Although no improvement in the condition of the people is apparent in the interior of the country, many changes have taken place in the capital itself during the past few years. The cars of the tramway run in the streets of Galata, the railway whistle is heard at the Seven Towers, and the ironclad floats upon the blue waters of the Bosphorus.* In nothing, however, has there been a greater change than in the social feeling and tone of thought of the Turkish women—a change which has been especially perceptible since

---

* It may perhaps be well to state that the tramway and the railroads have been made by foreign capitalists, and the ironclads were purchased with English money.

the visit of the Empress of the French in the year 1869. There is a great deal of misconception in England as to the status and treatment of women in Turkey. Most persons imagine that every Turk is more or less a Bluebeard, with four wives at least, and as many concubines to boot as he can well afford; the whole of whom are the mere slaves of his caprice, jailered by eunuchs, and without domestic authority of any kind. Nothing could well be farther from the reality. Instead of this paradisaic plurality being the rule, polygamy, in fact, is fast going out, in consequence of the expense which it entails. Odaliques, again, are the "luxury" of the very rich, and a very rare luxury too, for in Turkey, as here in the West, wives are jealous of their rights, and—whatever may have been the laxer rule in the good old times—they nowadays set their faces stoutly and successfully against illegitimate rivals. During my first visit to Constantinople, Fuad Pasha had the weakness to become enamoured with one of the female slaves in the harem, but, in a short time, he found it necessary to put the Bosphorus between her and his wife, and remove the former to another establishment at the village of Bebek. The Khanum is in reality as much mistress *chez elle* as any Western wife of the day, and has, if anything, more than her fair share of authority indoors. The Turks are, unhappily, not free from evils, many of which I have already described in a previous work, but there is one evil—the social evil—which has no home among them. The yashmak, feridjie, and shalwar, it is true, still hold their ground, but feminine coquetry has long since displaced the old opaque swathing, that hid everything except the eyes, for the diaphanous gossamer through which the whole battery of the wearer's charms now play as freely as if no single fold of muslin remained. The bright eyes flash and the pearly teeth dazzle beneath the veil, which, from the fineness of its texture, no longer serves to conceal, but rather adds an additional charm to the natural beauties of the wearer. The yellow papoosh, too, has largely yielded to the elastic European boot; but the Louis-Quatorze abomination is as yet foreign to the precincts of Stamboul.

The laws of the Koran give especial protection to women. No matter what political change may affect the husband, the property of the wife is always secure; under every circumstance it remains her own, nor is it liable for her husband's debts any more than the property of a married woman in England when secured by settlement. This, too, applies to all her property—not only that which she possessed before marriage, but also that which she may have acquired subsequently; while, if her husband purchase lands or houses in her name, they belong to her absolutely, and no claim of any kind against him can reach them. With us, paternity being ignored, the woman alone has the burden of natural children, and the shame of faults committed through passion; but according to the laws of the Koran, every woman that bears a child to a man has the right to claim the benefits of paternity for her offspring. The prohibition against wine and gambling, too, is a true safeguard for the wife against the brutalities of a husband. Drunkenness and gambling are the destruction of domestic peace, and, in cursing them, Islamism procures for the wife those positive guarantees which are in reality much more efficacious than the platonic recommendations of Christian preachers. Conjugal life is regulated by those words of the Koran (Chap. II., v.): "Wives should be obedient to their husbands and perform the duties devolving upon them, and husbands should treat their wives with justice, but they have authority over them." The Turks, however, did not make these laws. They are the laws of the Koran, which the Turks are bound to obey like every other Mussulman. The laws of the Koran were made by Mohammed; but Mohammed was an Arab, not a Turk!

The principal objects of interest to be seen in Constantinople are the Seraglio, or former palace of the Sultans, the Imperial Treasury, the tomb of Mahmoud, the old walls, the mosques, fountains, and bazaars. The Mosque of St. Sophia takes precedence of every other mosque, and is the most celebrated of all the edifices consecrated to the service of Islam. It was originally built by Constantine in A.D. 325, but, having been burnt down in the reign of Justinian, was rebuilt on a more splendid scale in the year 538. According to Von Hammer, the principal architects employed by Justinian in this masterpiece of architecture were Athenius, of Tralles, and Isidorus, of Miletus. A hundred other architects superintended the building, under each of whom were placed a hundred masons: five thousand of the latter worked on the right side, and five thousand on the left, according, as it was said, to a plan laid down by an angel who appeared to the emperor in a dream. The walls and arches were constructed of bricks, but the magnificence and variety of the marble columns surpassed all bounds. Every species of marble, granite, and porphyry—Phrygian, white marble, with rose-coloured stripes, which imitated the blood of Atys, slain at Lynada; green marble from Laconia; blue, from Lybia; black Celtic marble, with white veins; Bosphorus marble, white with black veins; Thessalian, Malusian, Proconessian marble, Egyptian starred granite, and Saitic porphyry—were all employed. The tiles on the arch of the cupolas, which astonished every eye by their extraordinary lightness and boldness, were prepared in Rhodes of a particular light clay, so that twelve of them did not weigh more than the weight of one ordinary tile. These chalk-white tiles bore the inscription: "God has founded it, and it will not be overthrown: God will support it in the blush of the dawn." When the building of the cupolas at length began, the tiles were laid by twelves, and after each layer of twelve tiles, relics were built in, whilst the priests sang hymns and prayers for the durability of the edifice and the prosperity of the church. The bringing together and preparation of the building materials occupied seven and a half years, the building lasted eight and a half years, and the finishing of the whole, therefore, took up sixteen years. When it was finished, and furnished with the sacred vessels, the Emperor, on Christmas Eve, in the year 538, drove with four horses from the palace above the Augustean to the church; 1000 oxen, 1000 sheep, 600 deer, 1000 pigs, and 10,000 cocks and hens were slaughtered; and during three hours 30,000 measures of corn were distributed among the poor. Accompanied by the Patriarch Eutychius, the Emperor entered the church, and then ran alone from the entrance of the halls to the pulpit, where, with outstretched arms, he cried, "God be praised, who hath esteemed me worthy to complete such a work. Solomon, I have surpassed thee!" When Constantinople was taken by the Turks, in May, 1453, the Greeks fled for refuge to the church of St. Sophia; but the gates were soon forced, and the carnage which followed was fearful. The dead covered the floor to the depth of many feet, and the massacre was only stayed by the entrance cf Mohammed II. himself, who exclaimed, "It is enough!" The grand Pan-Hellenic idea is, beyond everything else, the possession of St. Sophia, and the Greeks believe that the Cross will one day displace the Crescent on the minarets of their ancient church. It is well known that, at the commencement of the Crimean War, many Greeks postponed the baptism of their children in the hope that the triumph of Russian arms would enable them to perform this religious ceremony in the ancient basilicas which had been transformed into mosques. The other mosques worth a visit are those of Sultans Soleyman, Achmet, Bajazet, Selim, and Mahmoud, as also that of Eyoub, in which the Sultans are girded with the sword of Othman upon their accession to the dignity of Emperor and Commander of the Faithful.

The *Hasné*, or Imperial treasury, contains the rich collection of ancient armour and coats of mail worn by the Sultans, the most remarkable of which is that of Sultan Murad II., conqueror of Bagdad. The head-piece of this suit is of gold and silver, almost covered with precious stones. The diadem surrounding the turban is composed of three emeralds of the purest water, and of about seven to eight centimètres in size, while the collar is formed of twenty-two large and magnificent diamonds. In the *Hasné* there is also a curious ornament, in the shape of an elephant, of massive gold, standing on a pedestal formed of enormous pearls placed side by side. There is also a table, thickly inlaid with Oriental topazes, presented by Catherine of Russia to the Vizier Baltadji Mustapha, together with a very remarkable collection of ancient costumes, trimmed with rare furs, and, in some instances, literally covered with precious stones. The divans and cushions formerly used in the throne-room of the Sultans are superb, the stuff of which the the latter are made being pure tissue of gold, without any mixture of silk whatever, and embroidered with pearls weighing each about 3600 drachmas. Children's cradles of solid gold, inlaid with precious stones; vases of immense value, in rock-crystal, gold, and silver, enriched with rubies, emeralds, and diamonds; daggers, swords, and shields, beautifully wrought and richly jewelled—all tell a story of ancient wealth and grandeur, when the Ottoman Power was a reality, and Western Europe trembled before the descendant of Mohammed the Conqueror.

Among the principal "sights" of Constantinople are the "Howling Dervishes" at Scutari, and the "Dancing Dervishes" at Galata. The ceremonies of the former are, to my mind, rather repulsive, but those of the latter are exceedingly graceful and artistic. By far the most interesting sight, however, is that of the Sultan going in public state to mosque on Friday (the Mussulman Sabbath). It is a religious duty imposed on the Sovereign for the time being, from which under no pretence (unless in case of imminent danger from sickness) can he possibly be exempt. The present Sultan generally goes to the mosque at Béchiktach, a short distance from his palace at Dolma-baghtché; and long before the appointed hour the neighbourhood becomes thronged with a multitude of red-fezzed and turbaned men; whilst Turkish women, clad in snowy yashmaks, and glowing coloured feridjies of every shade, line the road at either side, from the grand gate of the palace to the mosque itself. A double line of guards keep the route, and at a few minutes before twelve a number of generals and colonels, riding two abreast, precede some files of superior officers on foot. Then come on horseback the principal ministers of state, followed by the Grand Vizier, and, at a short distance, the Sultan himself, mounted on a splendid Arab charger, richly caparisoned. Immediately behind His Majesty follow the body-guard, who are selected from the best families of every race in the empire, several led horses in magnificent trappings, and an escort of picked imperial troops. As the

Sultan passes along, the artillery at the arsenal fire one hundred and one guns, the bands stationed at intervals strike up the Sultan's March, and the soldiers shout, "Long live Abdul-Hamid! May he live for ever." It is a most imposing spectacle, and as the cavalcade of Pashas of every rank, with dazzling gold embroidery on their saddle-cloths, and uniforms studded with medjidies and nishan-iftiars, move down the line to the music of the imperial band, the *ensemble* compares favourably with any court procession to be seen elsewhere in Europe.

There are three routes by which the traveller can return to London. First, *viâ* the Danube to Vienna, stopping at Belgrade and Pesth; second, *viâ* Trieste, calling at Athens and Corfu; and third, by the French Messageries Maritimes steamer to Marseilles.

CHAPTER XVIII.

THE FUTURE OF THE OTTOMAN EMPIRE.

The Turks, as we have seen, still rule in the city of Constantine, and the Crescent still gleams on the minarets of Saint Sophia. The Turks, themselves, however, believe that sooner or later they will recross the Bosphorus;* and their ultimate retirement from Europe has been facilitated, in a most signal manner, by the Plenipotentiaries who signed the Treaty of Berlin. That treaty has left the Sultan little more than the city of Constantinople itself, together with a comparatively small garden in Thrace; and the force of circumstances will now oblige him to concentrate his attention upon those rich provinces in Asia which have hitherto been so neglected. The representatives of the Powers

---

* This traditional belief causes Moslems to order their bodies to be interred on the Asiatic side of the Bosphorus, that they may not be disturbed by the invaders.

met in the White Hall of the Radziwil Palace but to ratify foregone conclusions; the independence of Servia, Montenegro, and Roumania, and the detachment of Bulgaria, Bosnia, Herzegovina, and the Dobrudsha had been determined upon, and the result was the British Protectorate of Asiatic Turkey. As long as Turkey remained a Power in Europe, the idea underlying this Protectorate could hardly have been carried out, and the virtual dismemberment of Turkey was therefore consented to by our Government. It is true that that dismemberment could not have been long delayed, as the world had at length become aware of the inherent weakness and corruption of Turkish rule. This enlightenment was a long time coming to the British nation. We had read of the savageness of the Turk as a ruthless and licentious conqueror; but the day of conquest had passed, and the general notions of the Turk rested on the reputation of his former exploits. His critics, however, with a failing that leaned to virtue's side, appeared to forget the past, and assumed that his character had been modified, toned, and elevated by the influences of modern ideas and civilization. Never was there a greater delusion.

Born originally for an active life, to lead great herds into the steppes, and carry war and pillage amongst their neighbours, the Turks became enervated since the day when, driven back from the ramparts of Vienna, the sword fell from their grasp, and they retired to Constantinople, where they found their Capua. But, powerful to destroy, they have ever been powerless to construct. The social, religious, and political separatism which the dominant section of her population carried with them from the cradle of their race in Asia, remains as rigorously complete in the days of Abdul-Hamid as in those of Amurath I.; and their absolute infusibility with the conquered populations has shut out Turkey from those influences which might otherwise have raised her to a position of greatness, usefulness, and honour. The Turks assimilated many of the vices of Byzantine corruption, but they borrowed nothing useful or good from the civilization of Greece. After four centuries, they are to-day just what they were when they first left the plateaus of Central Asia. They have simply become effeminate without ceasing to be barbarous.

Although it may scarcely serve any practical purpose to search too minutely after the origin and causes of the delusions that existed in this country in reference to Turkish character, it is but just to state that successive administrations of Great Britain are largely responsible for these delusions, in consequence of a systematic policy of suppression of that information which, had it been given, would have rendered misconception impossible. Successive Ministries, led astray by diplomatic fictions which were dressed in the high-sounding phrases of pretentious statesmanship, talked grandly of "the balance of power in South-Eastern Europe," of "the integrity of the Ottoman Empire," of "the aggressive ambition of Russia," of "the dreams of Peter the Great and Catherine II.," of "the road to India;" and, arraying these phrases in loose order, contrived to impress Europe, and England especially, in favour of a foregone conclusion that would have shown no strength had its precise value been boldly challenged. "The integrity of Turkey" was the watchword adopted after this idle and misleading parade of fiction. "The integrity of Turkey" became the key-note of British policy; and, to justify this wretched programme, the ambitious designs of Russia upon Turkey in general, and Constantinople in particular, were repeated, in season and out of season, until it became almost an article of religious faith with Englishmen to believe in this chimera; and a part of their settled policy to resist it with all the might, authority, and power of Great Britain. The dissipation of these delusions produced a reaction. Englishmen refused any longer to be presented to the world as upholding the vilest oppression known to the present generation, and the result of this change in British public opinion may be found in the protocols of the Congress of Berlin.

Greece, unhappily, considers herself betrayed, as, relying on the promises of our Government, she remained inactive at the moment when her vital interests required energy and decision. But Greece has only herself to blame. When Servia and Montenegro declared war against Turkey in July, 1876, a treaty had actually been signed by which Greece bound herself to support Servia in arms. Servia and Montenegro, fully relying on the good faith of Greece, did take up arms, and confronted the full strength of the Ottoman power: but Greece proved recreant to her written pledges, and left her allies to fight their battles alone and bear the full brunt of Turkish vengeance. It was only after Russia had completely overpowered the armies of Turkey, under Osman and Mehemet Ali Pashas, that the Greeks crossed the frontier, hoping to snatch an easy victory from an already beaten foe. *Noblesse oblige;* and the men who write Leonidas, Epaminondas, and Alcibiades before their surnames, ought to have remembered that the glorious deeds of their ancestors could not be emulated when their own acts were tainted by weakness and dishonour. Thus it was that when Greece brought forward her claims before the Congress, these shortcomings, to give them no harsher name, were remembered against her, and she met with coldness in quarters where otherwise she would have found a warm and solicitous friendship. If the British plenipotentiaries had been sincere, they would have settled the proposed accession of territory to Greece by a protocol in the usual manner, instead of "inviting" Turkey to come to an understanding upon the subject. The Turk has little of the ancient Roman in his character, and rarely commits suicide. He would have submitted to the unanimous decisions of the Congress because his fatalism would have construed them as the decrees of Allah; but it is certainly rather hard that he should be compelled to perform the "happy despatch" upon himself. Whether or not that arrangements shall be made for a satisfactory rectification of frontiers in Thessaly and Epirus, the "Grand Hellenic Idea" is, I fear, destined to disappointment. Austria in possession of Bosnia and Herzegovina, and with a right of way to Salonica on the Ægean Sea, will ere long enter upon her destiny. Pushed out of Germany, she will inevitably become a Slavonic Empire, and will aspire to Constantinople, as her capital. Old Byzantium must ultimately fall either to the Greeks or the Slaves. With Austria at the head of the latter, and with a footing on the Ægean, there can be little doubt as to the result. Undoubtedly, there will be a struggle between the Greeks and the Slaves. The very air of Greece is haunted with memories of heroic deeds, and on her soil still dwell "sons of sires who conquered there." Another Botzaris may arise, inspired by the traditions of the past and aspirations for the future, who will lead his countrymen to the emancipation of the grand old land, and to the realization of their cherished hopes. In such a struggle, the Greeks might rely on a large and generous sympathy, and, perhaps, on even something more than barren sentiment.

Thus, in one way or another, the dominion

of the Turks in Europe is doomed; and British policy is now directed to strengthen the Osmanli in Asia, with a view to their becoming a powerful ally of England, and an important factor in the "Imperial Policy" of the British Government.

But the convention between England and the Sublime Porte—the principal outcome of recent British diplomacy in the East—is by no means invulnerable to hostile criticism; although it may, perhaps, prove in its ultimate significance one of the most important treaties of modern times. It involves issues which even its authors have probably not fully estimated—a reflection which does not enhance general confidence in the soundness of their policy, or the wisdom of this particular measure. It provides for the British protectorate of Asiatic Turkey under certain conditions; it is a treaty pregnant with great events, which may prove to be abortive, or which may develope into grand forces to dominate over the future history of civilization and religion. But what is this Protectorate which we have covenanted to assume under certain conditions? Roughly it may be said to be an agreement whereby Great Britain, on the one hand, undertakes to protect Asiatic Turkey from encroachment on its territory; and Turkey, on the other, undertakes to introduce reforms in her administration, and to purge herself of the scandals of misgovernment which have not only made her a bye-word among nations, but have been the cause of those external aggressions which have rent the empire asunder. That is to say, if the Sultan will henceforth fulfil his oft-repeated and as oft-broken vows; if he will enforce good laws, abolish corruption, dismiss the rapacious and sensual Pashas, and fuse into a happy and contented homogeneity the heterogeneous elements of alien races and hostile creeds; if, in fact, he will make Turkey in Asia a garden of Eden, then we will, on our part, drive off the Russian Bear, and protect the little Paradise Restored by all the force of British power. This cynical age will not fail to discover a strange incongruity in the terms of the mutual obligations of this treaty. The world is familiar with treaties offensive and defensive, and it is easy to understand how political considerations of reciprocal advantages might justify, or appear to justify, such time-honoured alliances; but how Great Britain is to find, in the mere amelioration of the Turkish Government, a justification for a contingent and lavish outlay of treasure and of blood, it is hard to conceive. In this case the sword and shield of Great Britain are offered as an incentive to virtuous government, and as a reward for respectable behaviour. The convention asks of Turkey no more than is already her duty to herself, to her people, and to her international obligations—a duty which she has shamelessly neglected, to the peril of European peace and at the hazard of her own extinction. What other nation, contemporaneous or historic, ever offered such benevolent protection? To what other nation, barbarian or civilized, would we, in the plenitude of our Imperial magnanimity, offer an alliance like this? Even the friends and admirers of the project have but little to say seriously in its behalf. Their advocacy is confined to exultation over its "Imperial grandeur." On the other hand, its enemies oppose it; partly because they suspect the quarter from which it has sprung upon the world, and partly, because they have a vague and misty perception of the terrible responsibilities which may follow in its train.

On the very threshold of our inquiry, and at the very entrance of the path that is to lead to the improvement contemplated by the convention, we are met with doubt, uncertainty, and difficulty. Does there exist any intelligent person so sanguine as conscientiously to believe that the Reforms which Turkey so blandly "promises" will ever be accomplished? She has promised them a thousand times, and a thousand times she has forfeited her plighted word. It would indeed be a grand consummation to see that land of boundless resources yielding her natural increase, to see her people grow happy and prosperous under the benignant smile of justice and freedom, to see the morn, and afterwards the day disperse the darkness of ages, and brighten up the scene with new hope, new life, new joy. But the dream will never be realized under Turkish rule, and at least one of the contracting parties will fail in his covenant, and thus release the other from his obligations. I write this with the telegram, "Constantinople, 17th October," before me to the effect that, "His Majesty the Sultan gave Sir H. Layard renewed verbal assurances of his acceptance of the British scheme of reforms in Asia Minor." But I have no faith in the promises of the Sultan. He cannot be a party to any scheme of reform which would be acceptable to the enlightened conscience of Western nations, all his "renewed assurances" to Sir H. Layard notwithstanding. The deep, abiding, and irrepressible corruption of his satellites renders it impossible; and the abuses, cruelties, and extortions of Turkish administration will only die with the hated race of Turkish administrators. In the preceding pages I have attempted by unimpeachable evidence to establish this painful and humiliating fact. But there is a fact even still more discouraging: Turkish rulers do not want reform, and they would not introduce anything worthy of the name even if they could. Men nurtured in the enervating atmosphere of harems, of intrigue and corruption have no appreciation for just laws and wise administration, nor have they any desire to rule over a contented and prosperous people. They have no interest in government except so far as they can make it minister to their cupidity and lust. All the higher aspirations after beneficent rule they consider to be chimerical notions for the amusement of the ghiaours, whom it would be profanity to imitate and whom it is religious to deceive.

It is only an idle dream, therefore, to suppose that Turkey will ever reform herself, or contribute, by anything like an honest fulfilment of her pledges, to the practical success of the convention as it now stands. It would be a wilful self-delusion to impose this belief on ourselves, as fidelity in this respect would be contrary to all the antecedents of the Turks. What then? Will the famous convention prove a diplomatic abortion, or, at best, fall still-born upon the world? If I understand aright its scope and design, it is not so intended. If I understand aright, the distinguished framers of the convention have themselves no belief in Turkish reformation; nor have they, on the other hand, any intention to abandon the "master policy" on which they have set their hearts, and to which they have to some extent already committed the nation. It is not their intention that a fiasco in Cyprus, and a fiasco in Asia Minor, shall be seen down the long vista of history like two weird witnesses pointing to the failure of British diplomacy in the nineteenth century.

It comes to this, then, since Turkey cannot and will not reform herself, will we feel ourselves bound, either by the terms of the convention or by considerations outside of it, to undertake the task ourselves? Are we so much in love with the reforms we desire, and so much impressed with our mission as to impose it on a reluctant Government, and enforce it by our own authority and power? If reforms are ever to be enforced, this is the only way by which the task can be accomplished. The real issue which we shall soon be called on to decide is —shall we accept the release from our engagement that Turkish incapacity will afford, and retire disgusted from the enterprise, or shall we assume responsibilites not defined in the convention in order to make our Protectorate a reality? We may be assured it is already determined, for good or evil, that we shall not retire, but that we are bound by the requirements of our Imperial policy to proceed.

We shall soon reach the critical point in the adventure, and must make our decision whether the new departure shall be to the right hand or the left. There was a former critical point when we stood debating whether we should enter on the path at all, but we elected to proceed. The past is irrevocable, and we cannot, therefore, dwell with any practical advantage on the decision which has been made for us by our rulers. I am indicating now the crisis of our future career. Shall we turn to the left hand, and again drag the policy of Great Britain along the dreary path of Turkish promises, and disappointed hopes? That would save us from many a peril, but it would scarcely be dignified for any Great Power to pace that weary round; as, apart from its inherent humiliation, it would lead us nowhere, and leave us with no other result than that the complicated maze of Turkish politics would become more and more involved, and the road more difficult to travel. If, however, we should determine to turn to the right hand, and undertake the initiation and confirmation of the reforms we consider essential, we shall enter on a path that will become more thorny every step we proceed, and beset at every stage with increasing difficulties, dangers, and responsibilities. It is important, therefore, that we should fully realize the obstacles and perils that await us, for, having once entered on the path, we must persevere with unflinching courage and undeviating resolution.

What would it involve for us to undertake the reformation of Turkey? Nothing less than to take into our own hands the whole administration of the country, in spite of the inveterate opposition and hatred of the ruling caste. It would mean that we should set aside for ever the incorrigible Pashas, abolish the hated tax-farmers, restrain the rapacious usurers, and, amid the unreasoning animosities of religious fanaticism, dispense equal justice between man and man, between Mussulmans and Christians. It would mean that we should appoint and maintain at their posts all the judicial and executive officers of state throughout the empire; with this difficulty, that foreigners do not understand Mohammedan law, and Mussulmans of the old school are so hopelessly corrupt that they will not apply it with equity. The first and essential requirement is a pure administration rather than new legislation. It is the administration which is so shamefully defective in Turkey; the law itself is in many respects just and equitable. But in purifying the administration, we should be met at every turn by the jealousy and obstructiveness of the officials; and the Turks are extremely sensitive and jealous, and masters in the art of obstruction. We could only accomplish this self-imposed task by reducing the sovereign power of the Sultan to a shadow, as we have reduced that of the rajahs of India. Such an encroachment on the prerogatives of the Sultan would be resented both by himself and any foreign allies which he might summon to his aid, and it is hard to say how many such allies jealousy of England might gather around him.

Now, if our Government are determined to make a reality of the British Protectorate of Asiatic Turkey, we shall be driven of necessity to repeat the steady aggression of our Indian career; and admirers of this Imperial policy will not be wanting in arguments to persuade us that this is at once our duty and our destiny. It is but seventy-five years ago that Wellington and Lake, in spite of themselves, and the restraints of Parliament and the country, began that onward and irrepressible march which has given us our colossal Indian Empire. Province after province we were compelled, or thought ourselves compelled, to annex in order to establish our rule, and preserve inviolate our authority over the districts previously under our sway. If we are to make the Convention anything but a dead letter, we must enter on the same programme of aggression and uncontrollable development in Turkey, and there can only be one end of that programme—the final absorption of the whole country, and the burden of its entire government.

During this century, in spite of our constant and, I dare say, honest determination to avoid further encroachments, conquests, annexations, and burdens, we have extended our Indian em-

P

pire till it reaches from Cape Comorin to the Himalayas and the Indus. At this very moment we are driven by an inexorable fate to fight with our neighbours the Afghans, and the probability is that we shall end by annexing their territory, which we affect to avoid rather than to court. But if this much has been done in a period of time comparatively so brief, what may not be effected in a similar period in the more northern theatre chosen for our future exploits? Nay, more: in this remarkable age, the acceleration of speed is measured by geometrical progression, and at this rate the whole face of the globe, or, at least, of Asia, may be changed in the next fifty or even twenty years. With Turkey in Asia annexed, Persia cannot long resist the sure process of absorption; and before men who are now young arrive at a sober maturity, "Asiatic Britain" may reach from the southern shores of the Black Sea to the southern point of the Indian peninsula. Incidentally, I may observe that every ancient invasion by India's conquerors set in from the north, and has been in due time swept away. Ours was first from the south and, though this may not be any guarantee for its stability, yet it may be the dream of Imperialism thence to extend our sway from south to north, over the ancient homes of civilization in Persia, Assyria, Phœnicia and Asia Minor, and thus consolidate an empire in the East, which neither Alexander nor the Great Moguls ever dared to covet. This dream has furnished, indeed, the key-note of the policy on which the country has been launched; this aspiration is the real motive of the convention between Great Britain and Turkey, all duly signed and ratified.

The grand conception is to create an "Asiatic Britain" greater than the one that has stood out so proudly and conspicuously in the history of centuries. But "grand conceptions" do not constitute statesmanship; they are very fascinating, it is true, but their fascination is apt to dazzle and mislead. They are like the treacherous *ignis fatuus* alluring us into situations of difficulty and danger; if we retrace our steps, we have to overcome again the perils through which we have passed, and which we have learnt to dread; if we proceed, we have to confront new dangers of which we know nothing, and which may be even greater than those we have escaped. Such a path is the one before us. It is one which no wise statesman, by free and deliberate choice, would adopt as the pathway of his country's career. We could only be justified in pursuing it if a stern necessity should be laid upon us. That necessity may come, and if it does, it will be our only justification. Had we kept out of Turkish entanglements, it is hard to see how such a necessity would have overtaken us; since we have committed ourselves to the grand work of Turkish reformation it is hard to see how we can escape it.

The supreme peril is found in the fact, that when the promoters of this Imperial policy shall have been removed, by death or by political changes, from the control of affairs, their opponents and successors will be compelled by *force majeure* to carry on the work which now they honestly and vigorously condemn. This policy will fructify in posthumous events, and its honour or dishonour will have a final development when its framers shall be gone. It is one that may, perhaps, yield a charm to adventurous spirits, but it will necessitate a mortal struggle, in which the great stake will be our Indian rule, and possibly the very existence of our Empire. And this is the policy we have avowedly undertaken in the defence of India, over whose teeming populations, it is said, we are to rule by the destiny of Heaven, and for the good of the Indian people!

The early incidents of the occupation of Cyprus supply a forcible illustration of the difficulties which will spring up with sinister and combative mien to confront us at every step, and dispute every inch of our march. The other day, the Chancellor of the Exchequer, in his speech at Birmingham, justified the acquisition of Cyprus on the ground that it would enable us to teach the Turkish community what reforms in the shape of administration and good government were expected from them; and he asserted that, setting aside military expenditure, the revenues of the island would pay the full charges of administration. I have shown that it would be a vain experiment to teach the Turkish Government by the force of good example; but even if it were an effort less equivocal, it would cost us both vexation and disappointment. Cyprus was to be an advanced post to strengthen our military and naval position in the East. Hitherto we have found it only a lazar-house and a grave for our soldiers; and authorities are divided as to any value it ultimately may possess if, after immense cost, we should at length convert it into an impregnable fortress. The island was, moreover, to be a new field for British enterprise; and the development of its resources, agricultural, pastoral, and mineral, was to give a new stimulus to our commercial activity and revive our languishing trade; but these hopes have not been realized. They were, in fact, absurdly sanguine, built on exaggerated estimates, and disappointment is the natural consequence.

It may be that, after a while, the trade of Cyprus will prove an appreciable item in the catalogue of British commerce. It may even be that for strategic purposes the island may prove useful in the further development of our interests and policy in the East. Time will show.

As to the insalubriousness of the climate, we may, by careful attention to the experiences we have acquired in various directions, succeed in banishing fever altogether, or in keeping it under effectual restraint. We may even destroy the conditions of its evolution by planting in sufficient numbers the *Eucalyptus Globulus*; for the rapid growth of this tree would doubtless convert the hotbeds of fever into beautiful forests of tall and aromatic timber trees. In Algiers and Italy, the experiment has been tried with success; and as for Australia, where this fine species is indigenous, that country probably owes the characteristic healthfulness of its climate to the prevalence of the "gum tree," which is the popular name of the *Eucalyptus*. At the Antipodes, by the absorption of the miasma and its transformation into a picturesque vegetation, this well-known tree has not only beautified the landscape, but it has been for ages preparing a healthful home for the settlers of our own times.

All these results may be attained in Cyprus, but it will only be after we have, at much cost of money, health, and life, triumphed over our difficulties, and achieved success. In like manner the Imperial policy, of which the occupation of Cyprus is the first experiment, may bring us to a final triumph in Asia; but it will be after unwonted prowess, terrible sacrifices, and efforts to be undertaken only by a Titanic race.

I may here take occasion to correct one mistake which has become prevalent. When reform in Asiatic Turkey is now mentioned, the geographical area is invariably limited to Asia Minor. But Asia Minor is only a part of Asiatic Turkey, and the convention, according to its exact terms, applies to the whole. What does this mean? That Asia Minor is the only part of the empire left free to the operations of our reforming zeal. France has been our faithful ally for many years, and she claims a prescriptive right to the protection of the Latin Christians in Syria and Palestine: so we have quietly dropped these "interesting countries," and the reforming spirit is to be confined to the districts of Asia Minor, with respect to which there are no particular European susceptibilities that we can wound. Yet, Syria and Palestine are sighing for emancipation, and, besides forming one of the fairest portions of the earth, they possess a native population of superior *physique*, of high intelligence, and every way worthy of the freedom they desire. No amelioration of Turkey will be complete which leaves them outside of its provisions. The sympathies of the people lean towards England; and I can confidently affirm that, if a plebiscite were taken to-morrow, the great majority of the populations, both Mussulman and Christian, would vote for annexation to the British Empire.

I cannot disguise from myself, and I have not disguised from my readers, the terrible responsibilities which the Protectorate will bring on Great Britain. Nevertheless it is incumbent on me to insist that, without the direct supervision of British administrators, all attempts at reforms will prove futile, and all procedure on any other basis will only be a mockery to the populations themselves. But whatever may be the contingent responsibilities on our own Government; it is certain that if the Sublime Porte were well advised, it would at once not only accept, but demand British intervention, for, otherwise, it will be powerless in the face of the opposition of the Ulemas, the Softas, the Dervishes, and of all those whose vested interests to plunder would be imperilled. No tottering Oriental or other Empire was ever before offered safety on the simple conditions now proposed to Turkey. But if the Turkish Government should refuse to accept this last chance, partition or annexation will become inevitable; and with the fall of the Ottoman Empire will come a new era of freedom and civilization for the down-trodden populations—Mussulman and Christian—of Asiatic Turkey.

APPENDICES.

APPENDIX I.

THE SUEZ CANAL.

THE 17th of November, 1869, witnessed the historical apotheosis of M. de Lesseps. After half a lifetime of devotion to an idea, and faith in his own destiny to carry it out, he, on that day, received a triumph grander both in its significance and its attendant incidents than Roman conqueror ever enjoyed. The presence, at the opening of the Suez Canal, of two sovereigns, half a dozen royal princes, statesmen, ambassadors, *savants*, and other celebrities beyond count—besides thousands of less distinguished visitors from the Old and New Worlds, and representative squadrons from every navy in Europe—sufficed to give an *éclat* to the occasion with which even a Frenchman's passion for "glory" might be well content. Nor was the honour unearned, for, be the mere commercial result what it may, this union of the two seas will rank amongst the great works of the world, and to M. de Lesseps, more than any other living man, does the credit of it belong.

Nor is this lessened by the fact that the idea which was thus realized is as old as the Pharaohs. Centuries before the Christian era, both Hebrew and Phœnician ships traversed the Red Sea on their way to Ophir, and, during the dynasty of the Ptolemies and the Roman dominion, large fleets were sent out annually from Berenice and Myos-Hormes to India. After the establishment of the Mohammedan Empire in the seventh century, an immense trade was carried on through the Red Sea with India and China; and, in the period between the twelfth and fifteenth centuries, the treasures of the East found their way over the coral-reefed Yam-Sûph to the Venetian factories in Alexandria. During the long historic span thus covered, many efforts had been made to pierce the Isthmus. Herodotus, Book ii., chap. 158, relates that Nichos, son of Psammiticus (616-600 B.C.), was the first who opened a communication by means of a canal between the Nile and the Red Sea. The canal was large enough to allow two trireme galleys to ago abreast, the water being taken from the Nile, a little above the ancient Boubrastis—subsequently called Basta—a city situated on the Pelusian branch of the river.

The canal opened into the Red Sea near the Pithomus of Scripture, the Patumas of Herodotus, and the Hieropolis of the Ptolemies, the site of which, at the present day, is to be found at the northern extremity of the Bitter Lakes, not far from the actual shore of the Red Sea. It must be remembered, however, that two thousand five hundred years ago those lakes were only an extension of the Erythrean Sea, and that the Gulf of Suez was then called the Gulf of Hieropolis. The galleys were towed by men, and Herodotus gives four days as the time required for the passage. It appeared, nevertheless, that this route was not the best, and that the most direct course would have been to begin the canal on the shore of the Mediterranean, near Mount Cassius, which separated Egypt from Syria, and from which the Erythrean Sea was only distant a thousand stadia. According to Herodotus, this was the shortest route. In cutting his canal, King Nichos caused the death of one hundred and twenty thousand men; but, having been told by an oracle that the canal would be the means of bringing the barbarians into Egypt, he discontinued the works, and gave up his project in despair.

According to Strabo, the canal of Nichos commenced at Phacusa, and passed to Belbeïs, where it met the one which washed the walls of Boubrastis. From Belbeïs (Pharbaetus), it entered the bitter lake below Hieropolis, and, as this canal was a derivative of the Nile, the water of the bitter lake, in receiving that of the river, partook of the character of the sweet water of the Nile. A century after Nichos, Darius, son of Hydaspes, King of Persia (521-485 B.C.) caused the works to be recommenced; but the engineers having assured him that the Red Sea was of a higher elevation than Egypt itself, he was so much afraid of altogether submerging the country he desired to improve, that the works were once more suspended. In fine, Ptolemy Philadelphus, King of Egypt (273 B.C.), finished the canal joining the two seas; and, in order to render the mouth of the canal in the Red Sea more safe, he made a dam (*hizei-orou*) which opened and shut at will. The dam served at the same time to collect the waters of the Nile in the canal, and thus facilitated internal navigation. The canal of Ptolemy entered the Red Sea near Arsinoé—the present Suez—which afterwards took the name of Cleopatra.

After the battle of Actium (31 B.C.), Cleopatra, seeing that the forces of Egypt could not resist those of the Roman Empire united against her, formed the singular project of taking her fleet through the canal into the Red Sea, and thus fly into some distant country. Some ships attempted the passage, but were burned by the Arabs, and Antony persuaded Cleopatra to abandon her design, and defend the entrance to her kingdom both by sea and land. Under the Roman Empire, Trajan renewed the canal of Ptolemy Philadelphus, and even added a branch which went some stadia below Memphis. This extension of the canal was called by the name of Trajan; Ptolemy called it Amina Trajanus; Quintus Curtius named it Oxius, and the Arabs *Merahemi*. Nothing further was done until the time of the Arabs, when, in the year 637 of the Christian era, Amrou, the lieutenant of the Khalif Omar, succeeded in reopening the old channel as far as Boubrastis, on the Pelusian branch of the Nile. Volney, however, relates, that one hundred and thirty-four years later the Khalif, Abou-Djaffat-el-Mansour, destroyed it in the hope of crushing his rebellious subjects by cutting off the means of transporting provisions, and thus starving them into subjection. From that time no further effort was made, and the canal soon became blocked up by the then unconquerable sands. So it remained for a thousand years, until, in 1798, General Bonaparte, commanding the troops of the French Republic in Egypt, proposed to cut a canal across the Isthmus capable of being navigated by sea-going ships, and the work, which had been begun upwards of two thousand four hundred years before, would then have been recommenced but for the mistake of French engineers, who declared the Mediterranean to be considerably below the level of the Red Sea, and a canal to be therefore impossible.

From that time the question continued to be agitated at intervals; but nothing definite was done till 1830, when Lieutenant Waghorn—then engaged in the establishment of his Overland Route—again surveyed the Isthmus, and found the level of the two seas to be identical. Still, though interest was for a time revived by the announcement of this fact, no further action was taken with reference to the scheme till 1847, when England, France, and Austria sent out a commission to solve, once for all, the problem of the sea levels. This commission—on which Mr. Robert Stephenson represented our own Government—confirmed Waghorn's report, with the sole variance of finding a difference of five feet in the tide—not the real—levels of the two seas at the proposed termini of the canal. Another examination, leading to similar results, was made five years later, but Mr. Stephenson nevertheless pronounced against the feasibility of the canal, and his opinion—though at variance with that of M. Talabot, the French member of the commission—being accepted by the Government and public of England, the railway from Cairo to Suez, which he recommended instead, was the result.

In the meantime another mind had been occupied with the scheme for nearly a quarter of a century. When Waghorn was advocating his own peculiar enterprise, young Ferdinand Lesseps was an *élève* in the French Consulate at Cairo, and, interested by our countryman's settlement of the sea levels, he conceived the idea of accomplishing the great work which, years before, Napoleon had abandoned. For four-and-twenty years of active official life the idea kept firm hold of his imagination, until being again in Egypt in 1854, he developed his plan to the then Viceroy,

Saïd Pasha, and finally, two years later, obtained from him a concession to construct a ship-canal across the Isthmus from a point near Tyneh to Suez. Of the opposition that then began on the part of Lord Palmerston and the English press it is needless to speak, for is it not all written in Blue Books and journals innumerable? This, however, rather stimulated than discouraged M. de Lesseps, while it also stirred up the national feeling in France, and, with its help, enabled him, in 1858, to launch his "Compagnie Universelle du Canal Maritime de Suez," with a capital of £8,000,000 sterling, on nearly every stock exchange in Europe. Few shares, however, were taken up out of France, but enough were placed there to warrant his commencing operations in the spring of the following year, and accordingly, on the 25th of April, 1859, the "Président Fondateur" and his little band of followers took possession, in the company's name, of the narrow belt of sand on the northern coast of the Isthmus, between Lake Menzaleh and the sea.

The subsequent ten years' history of the scheme need not be traced. Enough to say that, by dint of perseverance and energy, which may without extravagance be called heroic, M. de

Lesseps overcame difficulties against which few living men could have successfully battled, and he now has his reward in witnessing the completion of an enterprise which will indissolubly link his name with Egyptian history.—"*Modern Turkey.*" *By J. Lewis Farley.*

APPENDIX II

FUAD PASHA'S POLITICAL TESTAMENT.

To the Sultan Abdul Aziz.

[*Translation.*]

Nice, Jan. 3, 1869.

Sire,

I have but a few days, perhaps only a few hours more to live, and I wish to devote them to the accomplishment of a sacred duty. I desire to lay at the feet of your Majesty the expression of my last ideas,—sad ideas, the bitter fruit of a long and anxious career.

When this writing shall be placed under your Majesty's eyes, I shall no longer be of this world. On this occasion, therefore, you may listen to me without mistrust. The voice from the tomb is always sincere.

God has entrusted you with a mission as glorious as it is full of perils. In order to accomplish it worthily, your Majesty must endeavour to fully realize one great and painful truth—*the Empire of the Osmanli is in danger*.

The rapid progress of our neighbours, and the inconceivable faults of our ancestors, have placed us at the present day in an extremely critical position; and, in order to obviate a terrible catastrophe, your Majesty is bound to break with the past, and to guide your people towards new destinies.

Some ignorant patriots seek to make you believe that with our ancient means, we can re-establish our ancient greatness. A fatal error! an unpardonable illusion! True, if our neighbours remained still in the same state as in the days of our forefathers, our former means might have sufficed to render your Majesty the arbiter of Europe. But, alas! our European neighbours are far from being what they were. For the last two centuries they have all been moving forward, and all have left us far behind.

Certainly, we also have made progress. Your actual government is much more enlightened, and possesses much greater resources than that of your ancestors. But, unhappily, this relative superiority is far from sufficing for the requirements of our age. To maintain yourself in

Europe at the present day, you require not merely to equal, not merely even to surpass your ancient predecessors, but also to equal and proudly compete with your actual neighbours. To express my thought more clearly, I may say that your Empire is bound, under penalty of death in default, to have as much money as England, as much enlightenment as France, and as many soldiers as Russia. For us, it is no longer a question of making *much progress;* it is purely and simply a question of making *as much progress as the other nations of Europe.*

Our magnificent empire furnishes you amply with all the requisite elements for surpassing any European Power whatever. But to do this, one thing is absolutely necessary. *We must change all our institutions—political and civil.* Many laws, useful in past ages, have become injurious to society as it at present exists. Perfectible man needs to labour incessantly at rendering his own works more perfect.

Happily this first law of our nature is in entire conformity with the spirit of the Mussulman religion. For Islamism combines all the true doctrines which have for their essential object the progress of the world and the perfecting of humanity. Those who would assume, in the name of that religion, to enchain the onward march of our society, far from being Mussulmans, are but insensate unbelievers. All other religions are bound up with dogmas and unchangeable principles which are so many barriers against the progress of the human mind. Islamism alone, free from all the trammels of mysteries and infallible churches, renders it our sacred duty to advance with the world, to develop all our intellectual faculties to the utmost, and to seek instruction and the light of science, not in Arabia, not amongst Mussulman nations solely; but abroad, in China, to the farthest confines of the globe.

Nor must it be thought that Mussulman science is different from that of foreigners. Not so. Science is one. One and the same sun suffuses the world of intelligence. And as, according to our belief, Islam is the universal expression of all truths and all knowledge, so, therefore, a useful discovery, a new source of information, whencesoever it may have originated, amongst Pagans as amongst Mussulmans, whether at Medina or at Paris, belongs always to Islam.

Thus, nothing prevents us from borrowing the new laws and the new appliances invented by Europe. I have studied our religion sufficiently to discern its true spirit. I have my head still clear enough to weigh the value of my ideas; and, assuredly, it is not at the moment in which I am about to abandon life in order to present myself before the Supreme Judge of the universe, that I would venture to betray my Sovereign, my country, and my creed. I assure you, then, with the most profound conviction, that in all these institutions of which Europe gives us the example, there is nothing, absolutely nothing, contrary to the spirit of our religion. I solemnly declare to you that the safety of Islamism demands that we should adopt at once those great institutions *without which no Power can any longer exist in Europe.* I solemnly declare to you, moreover, that in thus transforming our empire, not only will you do nothing opposed to the holiness of our religion, but, by such action, you will render to all Mussulmans, the most loyal and legitimate, the most praiseworthy and glorious service that could have ever entered into the dreams of your most illustrious ancestors.

This great work of our regeneration embraces a multiplicity of questions which it is beyond my strength and the little of life remaining to me to dilate upon. But your Majesty has still at your side the eminent man whose friend and brother

I have been.* May God preserve him to you! for he knows better than any one the means of safety for your empire. I have never given your Majesty an advice without having previously satisfied myself that it was approved by his wise judgment, the fruit of his ripe experience. Continue, Sire, I beg of you, to give him your confidence. Accord it to him implicitly; for the confidence of great sovereigns constitutes the strength of great ministers. What I presume to recommend to your Majesty is—never to suffer the priceless talents of this devoted servant to be hampered by ignorant colleagues. Nothing could discourage him more than the necessity of working with men incapable of understanding him.

I must now say a few words with regard to our foreign relations. It is here that the task of our Government becomes truly disheartening. Being unable to contend with our enemies unaided, we are obliged to seek friends and allies abroad. Their various interests, at once jealous and hostile, unjust and powerful, have placed us in a position which it is impossible to portray. In order to defend the smallest of our rights, we are obliged to exert more strength, skill, and courage than our ancestors needed to conquer kingdoms.

* A'ali Pasha; died September, 1871.

Amongst our foreign allies you will find ENGLAND always in the first rank. Her policy and her friendship are as firm as her institutions. She has rendered us immense services, and it would be impossible to calculate those which she may render us in the future. Whatever happens, the English people, the most steadfast and the most wonderful in the world, will be the first and last of our allies. *I would rather lose several provinces than see the Sublime Porte abandoned by England.*

FRANCE is an ally that we must manage at all hazards. Not only because she can render us the most important services, but because she can give us also most deadly blows. With that chivalrous nation there is more of sentiment than calculation. She takes a pride in glory and great ideas, even with her enemies. Thus the best way to preserve the alliance of this generous people is to keep up with their ideas, and to realize such progress as will strike equally their imagination and their *esprit*. The day on which France will despair of our cause, she will herself bring about combinations hostile to our interest, and will end by causing our destruction.

AUSTRIA, embarrassed by her special European

interests, has been obliged up to the present to restrain her *rôle* in the East. She committed an immense fault during the war in the Crimea. Driven out of Germany, she will for the future see more clearly her danger from the North, and certainly that danger is not less perilous for her than it is for our own empire. As long as a firm and far-seeing policy rules at Vienna, Austria will naturally be the ally of the Porte. The great evil, the ever-recurring evil which has troubled the East during more than one century, will only be definitely eradicated by the active alliance of Austria, supported by all our other allies of the West.

As to PRUSSIA, she has been hitherto almost indifferent upon Eastern questions, and it is not at all improbable that in her hasty policy she may even sacrifice us to her own project of German unity. But it is quite certain that, after her unity is achieved, Germany will not be long in perceiving that she also has at least as much interest in the Eastern Question as any other European Power whatever. Still, God grant that she may not have purchased the spoils of Austria at the cost of inducing our enemies to irrevocably take possession of our European provinces.

I come at last to RUSSIA, that inveterate enemy of our empire. The extension of that Power towards the East is a fatal law of the Muscovite destiny. If I had been myself a Russian Minister, I would have overturned the world to have conquered Constantinople. You must not, therefore, be astonished at, nor complain of, the aggressive action of Russia. She acts towards us to-day, only under a new form, just as formerly we did ourselves to the Greeks of the lower empire. To guarantee us against Muscovite invasion, it will be, therefore, childish to rely solely upon our rights; what we want on that side is *force*. Not our old historic force, which we should try in vain to revive, but that new and irresistible force which modern science and ideas have placed in the hands of every European people. Since Peter the Great, Russia has made enormous progress, and soon her railways will double her power. That which alarms me most, however, is that, in Europe, the mass of the populations seem gradually to accustom themselves with resignation to the future encroachments of Russia.

The indifference of England to the events of Central Asia astonishes and alarms me. What alarms me most, however, is the considerable change which the pacification of the Caucasian provinces has brought about in the position of Russia. To me it is beyond doubt that, in any future events, the most serious attacks of the Russians will be directed against our provinces of Asia Minor. Your Majesty, therefore, should strive unintermittingly to organize our forces. Who knows if our allies will always be free to come in time to our aid? A domestic quarrel in Europe, and a Bismarck in Russia, might change the face of the world.

I can conceive of many acts of folly of all Governments; it is even one of their prerogatives to commit them. But I confess I have been unable to fathom the profound wisdom of the Governments which, with such strange indifference, permits the most frightful despotism in the world to put itself at the head of a hundred million barbarians, and arm them with all the appliances of civilization; to swallow up at every step provinces and kingdoms as large as France; and while it hems in Asia with its arms, and, on the other hand, undermines Europe by the agency of Panslavism, comes forward periodically protesting its love for peace, and its sincere resolution no more to seek for further conquests.

RUSSIA leads me to say a few words also of PERSIA.

The Government of this turbulent country, always swayed by Shiite fanaticism, has been the ally of our enemies from time immemorial. During the Crimean War it made common cause with Russia, and that it did not realize its hostile projects is owing to the vigilance of Western diplomacy. At the present day, the kingdom of the Shah is dependent on the Cabinet of St. Petersburg. So long as the Sublime Porte has her hands free, the Government of the Shah, feeble and ignorant as it is, without credit and without initiative, will never have the courage to seek a quarrel with us. But whenever we become involved with Russia, no matter with what care and consideration we may treat Persia, her political dependence, and, still more, her blind jealousy, will necessarily place her in the category of our bitterest enemies. Fortunately, in addition to our material resources, the Sublime Porte possesses moral means more than sufficient to keep in due respect a country crushed by a barbaric despotism, disputed by various pretenders, and, moreover, surrounded on all sides by Sunnite populations. On this point our interests are affected by many complex questions, which are entirely unappreciated amongst us, and which A'ali Pasha alone can explain to your Majesty.

Let us not forget GREECE—a country insignificant in itself, but an irritating instrument in the hands of a hostile power. European poets, in improvising this illusion of a kingdom, have thought they would be able to give life to a nation dead for the last two thousand years. In seeking to revive the country of Homer and Aristotle, they have only succeeded in creating a focus of intrigues, of anarchy, and brigandage. The Sublime Porte may find amongst the Greeks some intelligent servants; but the spirit of the Hellenic race will always be essentially hostile to our cause. The recollections of a glorious history, although separated from our Greeks of the present day by centuries of corruption, ignorance, and spuriousness, will yet for a long time foster amongst this selfish race the hope of juggling once again into existence the Empire of the East, which it formerly so degraded into the Byzantine Empire, or the *Lower* Empire, as it was so well termed. What guarantees us most effectually against the attempts of this false and spiteful people is its revolting vanity and exclusiveness, which render it, from day to day, more odious to all our Oriental races.

Our policy should be to endeavour to isolate the Greeks as much as possible from our other Christians. It is of paramount importance to withdraw the Bulgarians from the domination of the Greek Church, without, however, throwing it into the arms either of the Russians or of the Roman Clergy.

The Sublime Porte should never tolerate intrigues with a view to a union of the Armenians with the Orthodox Church. It would perhaps be wise to encourage amongst our Christians that philosophic spirit so well calculated to bring men into closer harmony by withdrawing them from clerical influence. But I hasten to add that, for us, the best policy will undeniably be to place the State above all religious questions whatever.

In our internal affairs, all our efforts should tend to one sole object—*the fusion of our various races*. Without such fusion, the maintenance of our empire appears to me an actual impossibility. Henceforward, this great empire can belong neither to the Greeks nor to the Slaves, to no single religion, nor to any single race.. The empire of the East can subsist only by the intimate union of all Easterns.

A powerful Germany; France with its forty millions of inhabitants; England strongly fortified as it is by nature—all these great nationalities may, indeed, for some time longer maintain their powerful and useful individuality. But a Montenegro, a principality of Servia, a kingdom of Armenia, without conferring the slightest advantage either upon themselves or the world, can never be anything further than States more or less chimerical, wretched fragments of former convulsions of humanity, inevitably a prey to any new conqueror, prejudicial to the progress of mankind, and dangerous for the peace of the world.

In the constitutions of modern States the only durable theory is that of great agglomerations. Thus, also, the only means of preventing the ruin of our State is to reconstruct it anew upon a broad and solid basis, embracing all our different elements *without distinction of race or religion*. Here we begin to encounter a somewhat serious difficulty. Our Christian populations, suddenly relieved from the sway which held them subject, seem too ready to replace their former masters. The Armenians especially have assumed an aggressive character; and it would be but right to moderate their ardour in opening our public careers only to such as shall have sincerely adopted the Unitarian principles of our empire. All our Christian populations have generally two distinct religions; one moral, and the other political. As regards the moral religion, our Government should ignore it completely; but, on the other hand, it should be closely attentive to all that relates to their political religion, for the latter often involves theories incompatible with our existence. In the fact of a Pasha worshipping God according to the law of Moses, or after the manner of the Christians, there is no reason why we should be deprived of the aid of his services. But if this same Pasha, oblivious of the unity of our country, indulge in dreams of a Byzantine empire, or aspire to serve a kingdom of Cilicia, then he ceases to be a faithful servant, and should be removed.

Unity of the State and of the country, based upon the equality of all—such is the sole dogma which I would wish to see exacted from all our public functionaries.

To elicit fully the marvels of this fruitful principle, your Majesty should apply yourself, in the first instance, to the organization of the *administration of justice.* The task is difficult, but it is urgent and indispensable. After having legally guaranteed the lives and property of all citizens, the foremost measure which your Government should consider as an imperious duty is the *construction of our roads*. The day on which we shall have as many railways as European nations, your Majesty will be at the head of the first empire in the world.

There is, however, another question which is for us of inexpressible importance—that of *Public Instruction*, the sole basis of all social progress, the perennial source of every moral and material greatness. Army, navy, administration are all involved in that. Without that essential basis, I foresee for us neither strength nor independence —neither government nor a future. Notwithstanding the eminently instructive spirit of our religion, education has remained very backward with us for a multiplicity of reasons. Our innumerable medressés, and the copious resources which are consumed by them so uselessly, supply us with the material ready to our hands for a grand system of national education. If I have myself failed to carry this fine thought into effect, it is because I have been diverted from it by a concurrence of most unfortunate circumstances. I bequeath the measure to my successors: they could not possibly conceive of any which would prove more fruitful or more glorious.

I know that the greater part of our Mussulmans will curse me as a *ghiaour* and an enemy to our religion. I forgive their anger, for they can understand neither my sentiments nor my language. They will one day come to know that I, a *ghiaour*, an "impious innovator," have been much more religious, much more truly a Mussulman, than the ignorant zealots who have covered me with their maledictions. They will recognize, but unhappily too late, that I have striven more than any other martyr to save the religion and the empire which they would have led to an inevitable ruin.

The first law of every institution, human or divine, is the law of self-preservation. And, in all our reforms, what have I sought but the preservation of Islam? Only that, instead of seeking it in blind submission to ancient prejudices, I have endeavoured to find it in those luminous paths which the God himself of Islam has traced before us, as he has traced them before all the nations of the earth.

My weak and trembling hand refuses to proceed further. In concluding these lines, I beg your Majesty will deign to give your attention to the dying words of a faithful servant, who, in the midst of human weakness, always loved his fellow-men, laboured constantly to accomplish all the good in his power, and who now, broken under the weight of his responsibilities, quits the world without regret, and dies a resigned Mussulman, delivering up his soul to the Supreme Judge, who is at once compassionate and merciful. —" *The Decline of Turkey?*" *By J. Lewis Farley.*

APPENDIX III.

LAW GRANTING TO FOREIGNERS THE RIGHT OF HOLDING REAL PROPERTY IN THE OTTOMAN EMPIRE.

WITH the view of developing the prosperity of the country, putting an end to the difficulties, abuses, and uncertainties which arise out of the exercise of rights of property by foreigners in the Ottoman Empire, and completing, by a precise regulation, the guarantees due to financial interests and administrative action, the following legislative enactments have been decreed by order of His Imperial Majesty the Sultan:—

Art. 1. Foreigners are admitted, by the same title as Ottoman subjects, and without any other condition, to the enjoyment of the right of possessing real property in town or country in any part of the Ottoman Empire, except the province of Hedjaz, on submitting to the laws and regulations which bind Ottoman subjects themselves, as hereinafter provided.

This enactment does not concern Ottoman subjects by birth who have changed their nationality, to whom a special law will apply.

Art. 2. Foreigners who are owners of real property, urban or rural, are consequently assimilated to Ottoman subjects in everything which concerns such real property.

The legal effect of this assimilation is: 1st. To oblige them to conform to all police or municipal laws and regulations which do now or shall hereafter affect the enjoyment, transmission, alienation, and mortgaging of lands. 2nd. To pay all charges and contributions, of whatever form or denomination, to which real property in town or country is or shall hereafter be made liable. 3rd. To render them directly subject to the jurisdiction of the Ottoman civil tribunals in every dispute relating to landed property and real actions of every kind, whether as plaintiffs or defendants, even when both parties are foreign subjects; in every respect by the same title and under the same conditions and the same forms as Ottoman owners, and without their being entitled in such cases to any advantage on account of their personal nationality, but with the reservation of the immunities attaching to their persons and their moveable effects under the terms of the Treaties.

Art. 3. In case of the insolvency of an owner of real property, the assignees under his insolvency shall apply to the proper authority and the Ottoman civil courts for an order for the sale of such of the insolvent's real possessions as are, according to their nature and the law, liable to the owner's debts.

The same course shall be taken when a foreigner obtains from any foreign court a judgment against another foreigner being an owner of real property. For the execution of such judgment upon the real estate of his debtor, he shall apply to the competent Ottoman authority for an order for the sale of the property liable to the owner's debts, and the judgment shall not be executed by the authorities and the Ottoman tribunals until they have satisfied themselves that the property proposed to be sold really belongs to the category of those possessions which can be sold to pay the owner's debts.

Art. 4. A foreign subject shall have the power of disposing by gift or will of such real possessions as the law allows to be disposed of under that form.

With respect to such real estate as he shall not have disposed of, or which the law does not permit him to dispose of by gift or will, the succession thereto will be regulated by the Ottoman law.

Art. 5. Every foreign subject shall enjoy the benefit of the present law as soon as the Power whose subject he is shall have assented to the arrangements proposed by the Sublime Porte for the exercise of the right of property.

Constantinople, 7 Sepher, 1284,
(June 18, 1867.)

PROTOCOL.

The law which grants foreigners the right of holding real property does not infringe on any of the immunities secured by Treaties, and which will continue to cover the person and moveable effects of foreigners who become owners of realty.

As the exercise of this right of property ought to induce foreigners to settle in greater numbers in the Ottoman territory, the Imperial Government feels it its duty to anticipate and provide for the difficulties to which the application of the law might give rise in certain localities. Such is the object of the arrangements which follow.

The dwelling of every person living on Ottoman soil being inviolable, and no one being allowed to enter therein without the consent of the master, unless in virtue of orders emanating from a competent authority and in the presence of the magistrate or functionary invested with the necessary powers, the dwelling of a foreign subject is equally inviolable, conformably with the Treaties; and no peace-officer can enter except in the presence of the consul, or a delegate of the consul, of the Power to which such foreigner is a subject.

By "dwelling" is understood a house of residence and its appurtenances, that is to say, the offices, courts, gardens, and contiguous enclosures, to the exclusion of every other part of the property.

In localities distant less than nine hours from the consular residence, the peace-officers cannot enter a foreigner's dwelling without the assistance of the consul, as stated above. The consul, on his side, is expected to lend his immediate assistance to the local authority, so that there shall not elapse more than six hours between the time when notice is given to him and the departure of himself or his delegate, in order that the action of the authorities may never be suspended for more than twenty-four hours.

In localities distant nine hours' journey or more from the residence of the consular agent, the peace-officers can, on the requisition of the local authority and in the presence of three members of the council of elders of the commune, enter the dwelling of a foreign subject without the presence of the consular agent, but only in case of urgency and to make investigations respecting crimes of murder, attempted murder, arson, robbery with violence, burglary, armed rebellion, base coining, and this whether the crime was committed by a foreign subject or by an Ottoman subject, and whether it took place in the foreigner's dwelling or outside it, or in any other place.

These regulations are applicable only to the parts of the property which constitute the dwelling as defined above. Outside the dwelling the police shall have free and unrestricted action; but where a person accused of a crime or misdemeanor is arrested, and such person is a foreign subject, the immunities attaching to his person shall be observed.

The functionary or officer employed to make

the domiciliary visit under the exceptional circumstances above described, and the members of the council of elders who assist, are required to prepare a *procès-verbal* of the domiciliary visit and to communicate it immediately to the superior authority under whom they act, who shall transmit it without delay to the nearest consular agent.

A special order will be promulgated by the Sublime Porte regulating the manner in which the local police are to act in the different cases above mentioned.

In localities distant more than nine hours from the residence of the consular agent, and where the law of the judicial organisation of *vilaets* is in force, foreign subjects shall be judged, without the assistance of the consular delegate, by the council of elders discharging the functions of justices of the peace, and by the tribunal of the *caza*, in disputes involving sums not exceeding a thousand piastres, or condemnation in a fine of not more than five hundred piastres.

Foreign subjects will have in every case the right of appealing to the tribunal of the *sandjak* from sentences so passed; and the appeal shall be heard and decided with the assistance of the consul, in conformity with the Treaties.

An appeal shall always suspend execution.

In no case shall the forcible execution of sentences pronounced under the conditions above specified take place except in the presence of the consul or his delegate.

The Imperial Government will issue a law determining the rules of procedure to be observed by the parties in the application of the preceeding provisions.

Foreign subjects in any locality are authorized to put themselves voluntarily under the jurisdiction of the council of elders or the courts of the *cazas*, without the consul's assistance, in disputes within the jurisdiction of those councils or courts, saving the right of appeal to the *sandjak*, which appeal shall be heard and judged with the assistance of the consul or his delegate. The foreign subject's consent to have his cause tried without the assistance of the consul ought in every case to be given in writing, and before any proceedings are taken in the cause.

It is to be well understood that none of these restrictions relate to processes or to questions affecting real property, which will be tried and decided according to the conditions established by the law.

The right of defence and publicity of trial are

assured in every case to foreigners who appear before Ottoman tribunals as well as to Ottoman subjects.

The preceding arrangements will remain in force until the revision of the old Treaties, a revision respecting which the Sublime Porte will hereafter endeavour to bring about an understanding between itself and the friendly Powers.

APPENDIX IV.

THE TRADE OF CYPRUS.

The following report by H.B.M.'s Consul at Larnaca on the trade and commerce of the Island of Cyprus, for the year 1877, has just been issued by the Foreign Office:—

SHIPPING.—There is a considerable falling off in the arrivals of British as well as of foreign ships, as compared with preceding years. The total amount of tonnage entered and cleared at Larnaca during the year, including the native coasting vessels, is 91,812 tons, against 92,926 tons for the year of 1876.* With the exception of an occasional French steamer, none but the steamers of the Austrian Lloyds' called here.

TRADE AND COMMERCE.—The depression of trade in Larnaca during the year 1877 is owing

* In 1877 total tonnage 91,812, of which 78,180 were foreign and 13,682 Ottoman. In 1876 total tonnage 92,926, of which 83,826 were foreign and 9100 Ottoman.

to the failure of the corn crops, on account of the continued drought during the months of January, March, and April, and to a considerable degree to the influence of the war. The want of rain also affected the culture of the locust beans and the growth of cotton. The imports for the year 1877 amounted to £105,277, as against £150,480 for the year 1876; and the exports to £150,981, against £207,512 in 1876.

GRAIN.—Although a very fair proportion of land was put under cultivation, the result of the grain crops for the year 1877 is as follows:— 800,000 kilos. of wheat against 1,600,000 in 1876; 1,500,000 kilos. of barley against 2,400,000 in 1876. Of this a little was exported in the early part of the harvest, and when it was thought that the crops would succeed better than they eventually did; as the season, however, advanced it was found necessary to import rather than to export, and prices of grain increased from £1 10s. to £2 15s. for wheat per quarter, and from 17s. to £1 12s. for barley per quarter.

COTTON.—The cotton crop in 1877 was very fair as regards quantity and quality, and may be estimated at about 2000 bales of 200 okes per bale, the average price being about fourpence per lb. Great care and attention are given to the cultivation of this plant, which is chiefly of American seed. Experiments have been made with the view of introducing the Bamia cotton, but it is thought the dry nature of the soil is little adapted for its growth.

Madder-Roots. — The produce in 1877 amounted only to about 250 tons. It is probable that the root will not be cultivated any longer, seeing that the expense of growing it exceeds the actual selling price. The cause of this is the late substitution of alizarine for madder roots. Prices averaged £12 per ton, free on board.

Wool.—The quantity of the wool produced last year was about 330,000 lbs. The mildness of the latter part of the winter, and the abundance of pasturage, greatly contributed to the growth of this article. The number of sheep is put down at 750,000.

Skins.—The trade in skins is somewhat brisk, though limited. Cyprus exports a certain number over and above its producing capacity, as some are brought from Egypt and other places to be prepared and tanned here. The prices were as follows: For lamb skins, 1s. 3d. each; for sheep, 8d. each; kids, 7d. each; goat,

1s. 3d. each; and for bullocks' hides, 1s. 3d. per oke.

WINE.—The manufacture of wine here is greatly on the decrease; for, owing to all sorts of unreasonable regulations and to the vexatious mode of their application, cultivators now prefer making their grapes into raisins. The wine produced in 1877 was 2,400,000 okes, of which one-fifth was commanderial. Prices of both, $2\frac{1}{4}$ piastres per oke first cost.

OLIVE OIL. — The produce in 1877 was estimated at 250,000 okes, against 200,000 okes in 1876. Prices ran from 9 piastres to 10 piastres an oke. The oil-producing districts are Keryina, Kythrea, Larnaca, and Limassol. As a rule, the olive tree only produces abundantly once in five years. The conditions required for a good yield are cold and wet weather, when the quantity produced may reach 400,000 and even 500,000 okes. It is rarely exported; when it is cheap, soap is made in such quantities as to supply Mersine and other parts of Caramania.

LOCUST BEANS.—The demand for caroubs being yearly on the increase, the peasants are seriously turning their attention to the proper cultivation of the tree, which was hitherto somewhat neglected. The yield in 1877 averaged 60,000 cantars of Aleppo, against 45,000 in 1876. It is most abundant when the winter is severe. In the early part of the season they changed hands at £3 5s. per ton, free on board. The last purchases were made at £4 per ton, free on board.

TOBACCO.—The monopoly is farmed out, and there are eight depôts in the island, of which four are in Nicosia, two in Larnaca and two in Limassol, opened in 1874. Selling prices vary from 30 to 10 piastres. The quality sold here is principally the lowest, and about 6000 okes, at 15 piastres the oke. The quantity disposed of in a year is about 100,000 okes, from which the Government nets 1,300,000 paistres. The payment to the Government was formerly made in medjidis, at 20 piastres, but now caïmé is taken at par. Of the above quantity of 100,000 okes, one-tenth is exported to Syria and Caramania in sealed packets. The tobacco used here is brought from Volo and Salonica, where it pays an "octroi" duty of three piastres per oke. Cyprus formerly produced about 200,000 okes of tobacco; but now, on account of the vexations to which the grower is subjected, the quantity grown does not exceed 5000 okes.

SILK.—The production of silk has sensibly

diminished during the last few years, owing to disease among the silk-worms, and to a partial fall in prices in the French market. The quantity produced formerly exceeded 25,000 okes of reeled silk. In 1877 the estimate of dry cocoons exported is 15,000 okes, and of those used in the island 4000 okes. Price of cocoons 3s. 6d. per lb., free on board.

SALT.— The salt lakes of Larnaca, which belong to the Government, can produce salt to the extent of 20,000,000 okes per annum. It is collected in the autumn, and sells at 20 paras per oke in caimé. In 1877 the quantity exported, principally to Syria, amounted to 3,734,000 okes, and that for internal consumption is estimated at 729,000 okes, making a total of 4,463,000 okes.

SPONGES.—Sponge fishing commences in May and ends in August. The fishers are Greeks from the islands of Hydra and Castelrossa. About forty boats in all were employed in 1877, each boat being manned by a crew of eight to ten. Operations extend from Baphos to Caravostassi, on the south-western and western coasts, and Famagusta to Cape St. Andrea, on the eastern coast. The quantity taken last summer amounted to about 2500 okes, of all sizes and qualities, chiefly of the more common kind. 500 okes were sold to Syrian buyers at 20 francs per oke; the remainder were taken away.

POPULATION.—The population of Cyprus is estimated at 200,000, of which about two-thirds are Greeks, with few exceptions, and the remainder are Moslems.

INDUSTRY.—Tanning is one of the chief industries. The tanneries at Nicosia turn out from 1500 to 2000 bales of leather per annum. The manufacture of silk stuffs is produced at Nicosia by women to the extent of about 10,000 pieces yearly for dresses, besides handkerchiefs and sashes. The printing of English grey cloths for divans and coverlets is also carried on; building and carpentering are entirely done by Greeks, who also make good tailors and shoemakers. The trades followed by Turks are those of barbers, butchers, calico-printers, shoemakers, and saddlers.

REVENUE.—The revenues for the financial year of 1877 are considerably under those of last year, in consequence of the unfavourable returns of the crops. The tithes were administered by Government officials, with a view to remedy certain abuses complained of by the peasants; but the experiment so far has not benefited either them or the Government. Of the dimes in grain 120,000 kilos. of barley were sent to Constantinople for the requirements of the army, and a matter of 30,000 kilos. of wheat were given to the poorer of the peasants for sowing.

PUBLIC WORKS AND ADMINISTRATION.—Nothing has been done in the way of public works during the year, even the carriage-road between Larnaca and Nicosia, which was traced out a few years ago at a great outlay, has been greatly neglected. No other roads exist in the island save bridle paths, some of which are also used by bullock carts. There are no wharfs and jetties. The only facilities for shipping are a few wooden scalas, and these, as a rule, generally disappear in winter. The promised reforms have not yet been applied to this island. The peasants continue to be heavily taxed, and as their ability to pay has diminished, arbitrary measures are resorted to for their collection. The Government does not seem to have been very fortunate in the selection of its administrative and judicial officials for Cyprus, and as complaints have been made against some of them the vali of Rhodes sent a functionary, accompanied by an efficient staff, to make the necessary investigations.

CUSTOM HOUSE.—Complaints were lately made

against the director of the Larnaca custom house because he insisted that all produce exported from this town should pass through the custom house instead of being shipped as formerly from the different scalas under the supervision of a custom house clerk, and after the required formalities of weighing, &c., had been gone through. As this was an impossibility, owing to the smallness of the building and the limited space in front of it, confusion and delay ensued, to the prejudice of the merchants and of the Government. This state of things having been brought to the notice of the superior authorities of Indirect Contributions at Constantinople, an inspector was sent over from Beyrout to make a full and complete report of the grievances complained of. No result has come of it as yet.

MR. LEWIS FARLEY.

MR. LEWIS FARLEY.

(TRANSLATED FROM "THE GOLOS.")

Mr. Lewis Farley is one of those men whom Horace calls *justum et tenacem propositi virum;* one of those men who do honour to their country, and consider it a duty to contribute to the welfare of mankind. When we meet with such men, it is impossible not to speak of them, and when we see their acts, it is impossible not to respect them. It is in the nature of such men to seek the truth, and the truth once discovered, neither obstacles nor personal considerations can turn them. Mr. Farley was brought up under the influence of English traditions, and with the *parti pris* of a citizen of Great Britain. In his youth, he had faith in Turkey, and distrusted Russia— demi-barbarous, unprogressive, tyrannous, and a dangerous foe to the progress and the civilization of Europe. He was sincerely convinced that it was the duty of England to defend Turkey against her covetous neighbour, and he sincerely admired Fuad and A'ali Pashas as the representatives of a civilized and regenerated Turkey. Mr. Farley had held a distinguished post in the Ottoman Bank, and was also a Turkish consul; he travelled in Turkey, and wrote letters to the English newspapers, full of Turkish sympathies; he published two works, "The Resources of Turkey" and "Modern Turkey," with the view of proving that the natural resources of Turkey were inexhaustible, and that the germs of civilization only required to be cultivated. . . . Nevertheless, truth was before everything else with him, and, even in 1860, when he was on terms of personal friendship with Fuad and A'ali, he could not help seeing clearly what was passing around him, and he hesitated not to say frankly what he thought. In his letters published at the time in the "Morning Post," he showed that the disturbances in Syria were provoked, not by the Christians but by the Turks. Those letters caused a rupture between him and Sir Henry Bulwer, then British ambassador at Constantinople, and so displeased Lord Palmerston that the Editor of the "Morning Post" requested Mr. Farley to discontinue his correspondence. In his book, "The Massacres in Syria," published in 1861, Mr. Farley graphically and truthfully described to the English public the horrors and the crimes committed in Syria by the Turks.

As long as Fuad and A'ali Pashas lived, Mr. Farley continued to believe in the possibility of a regenerated Turkey, but upon the death of those statesmen, his illusions gradually vanished. In January, 1875, before the insurrection in Bosnia had broken out, he published a pamphlet, "The Decline of Turkey," in which he predicted not only the bankruptcy of the Ottoman Government, which took place in the following month of October, but the other principal events that Europe has since witnessed. For many Englishmen, however, this book was written too soon. Few could bring themselves to believe in the near approach of the decadence of Turkey, not even when Bosnia and the Herzegovina were in flames. Little attention was paid to the condition of the Christians, who were considered simply in the light of revolted subjects of the Sultan, and many persons desired the speedy suppression of the revolt, which they believed to be directed against the sovereign rights of the Sublime Porte. Mr. Farley made an effort to show his compatriots to what extent they were deceiving themselves, and endeavoured to prove the culpability of the Ottoman Government, and, at the same time, arouse a sympathy for the oppressed Christians. His first public meeting was attended by not more than fifty persons, and even the press derided his attempt. Mr. Farley, however, was not discouraged. In December, 1875, he founded "The League in Aid of the Christians of Turkey," the object of which was to relieve the sufferings of the Rayahs; and he sought the co-operation of all those whom he thought likely to understand the ends he had in view.

At first the success of "The League" was not much better than that of the "meeting" to which we have alluded. But the movement in the East of Europe soon assumed greater extension, and Servia and Montenegro took up arms. The indefatigable Mr. Farley published another book, "Turks and Christians," in which he demonstrated the true character of the Ottoman Government, and faithfully described the sufferings of the Christians, all based upon facts of which he had been a witness during a long residence in the East. This book made a great impression, and immensely contributed to the development of the League. Public meetings were held in Manchester, Birmingham, Darlington, Edinburgh, &c., and, in July, 1876, The League was so powerful that Lord Derby recognized its authority, and received a deputation from its members. A great public meeting was shortly after held in London, which was a triumph for The League. The name of Lord Russell was on the list of patrons. Lord Shaftesbury occupied the chair, and fifty Members of Parliament gave in their adherence, of whom twenty-five occupied seats on the platform. . . .

After all we have said, it will be easy for our readers to see how much Mr. Farley has contributed to the success of the great work, and what a great *rôle* he has sustained in the movement which has enlisted the sympathies of the English people for the Christians of the East.

www.ingramcontent.com/pod-product-compliance
Lightning Source LLC
Chambersburg PA
CBHW032113230426
43672CB00009B/1719